James Thomson Callendar

**The Political Progress of Britain**

James Thomson Callendar

**The Political Progress of Britain**

ISBN/EAN: 9783744760577

Printed in Europe, USA, Canada, Australia, Japan

Cover: Foto ©ninafisch / pixelio.de

More available books at **www.hansebooks.com**

THE

# POLITICAL PROGRESS

OF

# BRITAIN;

OR, AN

## IMPARTIAL HISTORY

OF

### ABUSES in the GOVERNMENT

OF THE

### British Empire,

IN

## EUROPE, ASIA, AND AMERICA,

FROM THE

### REVOLUTION IN 1688,

TO THE

### PRESENT TIME.

*The whole tending to prove the ruinous Consequences of the popular System*

OF

### TAXATION, WAR, AND CONQUEST.

_____

" THE WORLD'S MAD BUSINESS."

_____

*PHILADELPHIA:*

PRINTED FOR J. T. CALLENDER.

# ADVERTISEMENT.

THE First Edition of *The Political Progress of Britain* was published at Edinburgh and London, in Autumn, 1792. The sale was lively, and the prospect of future success flattering. The plan was, to give an impartial history of the abuses in government, in a series of pamphlets. But while the author was preparing for the press, a second number, along with a new edition of the first, he was, on the 2d of January, 1793, apprehended, and with some difficulty made his escape. Two bookfellers, who acted as his editors, were profecuted ; and after a very arbitrary trial, they were condemned, the one to three months, and the other to fix months of imprifonment. A revolution will take place in Scotland before the lapfe of ten years at fartheft, and moft likely much fooner. The Scots nation will then certainly think itfelf bound, by every tie of wifdom, of gratitude, and of juftice, to make reparation to thefe two honeft men, for the tyranny which they have encountered in the caufe of truth. In Britain, authors and editors of pamphlets have long conducted the van of every revolution. They compofe a kind of forlorn hope on the fkirts of battle : and though they may often want experience, or influence, to marfhal the main body, they yet enjoy the honour and the danger of the firft rank, in ftorming the ramparts of oppreffion.

A copy of the firft edition was handed to Mr. Jefferfon, late American Secretary of State. He fpoke of it, on different occafions, in refpectful terms. He faid that it contained " the moft aftonifhing concentration of abufes that he had " ever heard of in any government." He inquired, why it was not printed in America ? and faid, that he, for one, would gladly become a purchafer. Other gentlemen have delivered their opinions to the fame effect ; and their encouragement was one caufe for the appearance of this American edition.

The

The work is intended for that clafs of people who has
not much time to fpend in reading, and who wants a plain
but fubftantial meal of political information. The facts are,
therefore, crowded together as clofely as poffible. All the co-
quetry of authorfhip has been avoided. The ambition of the
writer was to be candid, unaffected, and intelligible; becaufe truth is the bafis of found argument, fimplicity the foul
of elegance, and perfpicuity the fupreme touch-ftone of accu-
rate compofition.

A report was circulated, and believed, in Scotland, that this
production came, in reality, from the pen of one of the judges
of the court of feffion. The charge was unjuft. His lordfhip
did not write a fingle page of it; but he faid openly, that its
contents were authentic, and unanfwerable; and that the public were welcome to call it his.

For the extreme rafhnefs of his plan, the writer cannot offer an apology that prudence will accept. A fhort ftory
may, perhaps, convey the motives of his conduct. In 1758,
the Duke of Marlborough, with eighteen thoufand men landed
on the coaft of France. The troops, when difembarking, were
oppofed by a French battery, which was immediately filenced,
for it confifted only of an old man, armed with two mufkets;
he was flightly wounded in the leg, and made prifoner. The
Englifh afked him, whether he expected that his two mufkets
were to filence the fire of their fleet? "Gentlemen," he replied,
" I have done only my duty, and if all my countrymen here
" had acted like me, you would not this day have landed at
" Concale."

JAMES THOMSON CALLENDER,
*An Exile for writing this Pamphlet.*

Philadelphia, March 31, 1795.

# INTRODUCTION.

WITHIN the laſt hundred years of our hiſtory, Britain has been five times at war with France, and ſix times at war with Spain. During the ſame period, ſhe has been engaged in two rebellions at home, beſides an endleſs catalogue of maſſacres in Aſia and America. In Europe, the common price which we advance for a war, has extended from one to three hundred thouſand lives, and from ſixty to an hundred and fifty millions ſterling. From Africa, we import annually between thirty and forty thouſand ſlaves, which riſes in the courſe of a century to at leaſt three millions of murthers. In Bengal only, we deſtroyed or expelled, within the ſhort period of ſix years, no leſs than five millions of induſtrious and harmleſs people *; and as we have been ſovereigns in that country, for above thirty-five years, it may be reaſonably computed that we have ſtrewed the plains of Indoſtan with fifteen or twenty millions of carcaſes. If we combine the diverſified ravages of famine, peſtilence, and the ſword, it can hardly be ſuppoſed, that in theſe tranſactions leſs than fifteen hundred thouſand of our countrymen have periſhed; a number equal to that of the whole inhabitants of Britain who are at preſent able to bear arms. In Europe, the havock of our antagoniſts has been at leaſt not inferior to our own, ſo that this quarter of the world alone has loſt by our quarrels, three millions of men in the flower of life; whoſe deſcendants, in the progreſs of domeſtic ſociety, would have ſwelled into multitudes beyond calculation. The perſons poſitively deſtroyed muſt, in the whole, have exceeded twenty millions, or two hundred thouſand acts of homicide *per annum*. Theſe victims have been ſacrificed to the balance of power, and the balance of trade, the honour of the Britiſh flag, the univerſal ſupremacy of par-

---

* Infra, chap. 1.

liament,

liament, and the security of the Protestant succession. If we are to proceed at this rate for another century, we may, which is natural to mankind, admire ourselves, and our atchievements, but every other nation in the world must have a right to wish that an earthquake or a volcano may first bury both islands together in the centre of the globe ; that a single, but decisive exertion of Almighty vengeance may terminate the progress and the remembrance of our crimes.

In the scale of just calculation, the most valuable commodity, next to human blood, is money. Having made a gross estimate of the destruction of the former, let us endeavour to compute the consumption of the latter. The war of 1689 cost sixty millions of public money, and at the end of it, the public debts amounted to twenty millions, or by another account*, to be seventeen millions and a half; so that not more than one third part of the expences were *borrowed*. In Queen Anne's war, forty or fifty millions sterling were also sunk in the same manner, besides about thirty millions, which were added to the former public debt. Very large sums have since been absorbed in other wars, over and above those which were placed to the national credit. In 1783, by the report of the commissioners of public accounts, the total debts of Britain extended to two hundred and seventy-nine millions, six hundred and ninety-eight thousand pounds, though many millions have been paid off in time of peace, by what is called the sinking fund. Hence we see, that this sum of *two hundred and seventy-nine millions* is much inferior to the actual charges of these wars. The total amount may be fixed somewhere perhaps between four and six hundred millions. To this we must subjoin the value of sixteen or twenty thousand merchant ships taken by the enemy. This diminutive article of fixty or an hundred millions would have been sufficient for transporting and settling eight or twelve hundred thousand farmers, with their families, on the banks of the Potowmack or the Missisippi. By the report above quoted, we learn, that in 1783, the interest of our public debts ex-

---

* Memoirs of Britain and Ireland, vol. ii.

tended

tended to nine millions, and five hundred thousand pounds, which is equivalent to an annual tax of twenty shillings *per* head, on every inhabitant of Britain. The friends of our intelligent and respectable minister, Mr. Pitt, make an infinite bustle about the nine millions of debt which his ingenuity has discharged. They ought to arrange, in an opposite column, a list of the additional taxes which have been imposed, and of the myriads of families, whom such taxes have ruined. At best, we are but as a person transferring his money from the right pocket to the left. Perhaps a Chancellor of the Exchequer might as well propose to empty the Baltick with a tobacco-pipe. Had the war with America lasted for two years longer, Britain would not at this day have owed a shilling; and if we shall persist in rushing into carnage, with our former contempt of all feeling and reflection, it may still be expected that, according to the practice of other nations, a sponge or a bonfire will finish the game of funding.

What advantage has resulted to Britain from such incessant scenes of prodigality and of bloodshed? In the wars of 1689, and 1702, this country was neither more nor less than an hobby horse for the Emperor and the Dutch. The rebellion in 1715 was excited by the despotic insolence of the Whigs. The purchase of Bremen and Verden produced the Spanish war of 1718, and a squadron dispatched for six different years to the Baltick. Such exertions cost us an hundred times more than these quagmire Dutchies are worth, even to the Elector of Hanover; a distinction which on this business becomes necessary, for as to Britain, it was never pretended, that we could gain a farthing by such an acquisition. In 1727, the nation forced George the First into a war with Spain, which ended as usual with much mischief on both sides. The Spanish war of the people in 1739, and the Austrian subsidy war of the crown, which commenced in 1741, were absurd in their principles, and ruinous in their consequences. At sea, we met with nothing but hard blows. On the continent, we began by hiring the Queen of Hungary to fight her own battles against the King of Prussia; and ten years after the war ended, we hired the King of Prussia

with

with ſix hundred and ſeventy-one thouſand pounds *per annum,*
to fight his own battles againſt her.  If this be not folly, what
are we to call it ?  As to the quarrel of 1754,  " It was re-
" marked by all Europe," ſays Frederick, " that in her diſpute
" with France, *every wrong ſtep was on the ſide of England."*
By nine years of butchery, and an additional debt of ſeventy
millions ſterling, we ſecured Canada ; but had Wolfe and his
army been driven from the heights of Abraham, our grandſons
might have come too early to hear of an American revolution.
As to this event, the circumſtances are too ſhocking for reflection.  At that time an Engliſh woman had diſcovered a remedy
for the canine madneſs, and Frederick adviſes a French cor-
reſpondent *to recommend this medicine to the uſe of the Parliament
of England, as they muſt certainly have been bitten by a mad dog.*

In the quarrels of the Continent we ſhould concern ourſelves
but little ; for in a defenſive war, we may ſafely defy all the
nations of Europe.  When the whole civilized world was em-
bodied under the banners of Rome, her Dictator, at the head of
thirty thouſand veterans, diſembarked for a ſecond time on the
coaſt of Britain.  The face of the country was covered with a
foreſt, and the ſolitary tribes were divided upon the old queſtion, *Who ſhall be king ?*  The iſland could hardly have attained
to a twentieth part of its preſent population, yet by his own
account, the invader found a retreat prudent, or perhaps neceſſary.  South Britain was afterwards ſubjected, but this acquiſi-
tion was the taſk of centuries.  Every village was bought with
the blood of the legions.  We may confide in the moderation
of a Roman Hiſtorian, when he is to deſcribe the diſaſters of
his countrymen.  In a ſingle revolt, eighty thouſand of the
uſurpers were extirpated ; and fifty, or, as others affirm, ſeventy
thouſand ſoldiers periſhed in the courſe of a Caledonian campaign.  Do the maſters of modern Europe underſtand the art of
war better than Severus, and Agricola, and Julius Cæſar ?  Is
any combination of human power to be compared with the ta-
lents and reſources of the Roman empire ?  If our naked anceſtors reſiſted and vanquiſhed the conquerors of the ſpecies,
what have we to fear from any antagoniſt of this day ?  On ſix
months

months warning we could muster ten or twelve hundred thousand militia. Yet, while the despots of Germany were fighting about a suburb, the nation has condescended to tremble for its existence, and the blossoms of domestic happiness have been blasted by subsidies, and tide-waiters, and press-gangs, and excisemen. Our political and commercial systems are evidently nonsense. We possess within this single island, every production, both of art and nature, which is necessary for the most comfortable enjoyment of life ; yet for the sake of tea, and sugar, and tobacco, and a few other despicable luxuries, we have rushed into an abyss of blood and taxes. The boasted extent of our trade, and the quarrels and public debts which attend it, have raised the price of bread, and even of grass, at least three hundred *per cent*.

This pamphlet consists not of fluent declamation, but of curious authenticated and important facts, with a few short observations interspersed, which seemed necessary to explain them. The reader will meet with no mournful periods to the memory of *annual* or *triennial* parliaments ; for while the members are men such as their predecessors have almost always been, it is but of small concern whether they hold their places for life, or but for a single day. Some of our projectors are of opinion, that to shorten the duration of parliament would be an ample remedy for all our grievances. The advantages of a popular election have likewise been much extolled. Yet an acquaintance with Thucydides, or Plutarch, or Guicciardini, or Machiavel, may tend to calm the raptures of a republican apostle. The plan of universal suffrages has been loudly recommended by the Duke of Richmond ; and, on the 16th of May 1782, that nobleman, seconded by Mr. Horne Tooke, and Mr. Pitt, was sitting in a tavern, composing advertisements of reformation for the newspapers. MUTANTUR TEMPORA. But had his plan been adopted, it is possible that we should at this day, have looked back with regret, on the humiliating yet tranquil despotism of a Scots, or a Cornish borough.

The style of this work is concise and plain ; and it is hoped that it will be found sufficiently respectful to all parties. The queſtion to be decided is, are we to proceed with the war ſyſtem? Are we, in the progreſs of the nineteenth century, to embrace five thouſand freſh taxes, to ſquander a ſecond five hundred millions ſterling, and to extirpate twenty millions of people?

THE

# POLITICAL PROGRESS

OF

# BRITAIN.

---

## CHAPTER I.

---

Dutch prowefs, Danifh wit, and Britifh policy,
Great NOTHING ! mainly tend to thee.   ROCHESTER.

THE people of Scotland are, on all occafions, foolifh enough
to intereft themfelves in the good or bad fortune of an
Englifh minifter; though it does not appear that we have more
influence with fuch a minifter, than with the cabinet of Japan.
To England we were for many centuries a hoftile, and we are
ftill confidered by them as a foreign, and in effect a conquered
nation.   It is true, that we elect very near a twelfth part of the
Britifh Houfe of Commons; but our reprefentatives have no
title to vote, or act in a feparate body.   Every ftatute proceeds
upon the majority of the voices of the whole compound affembly : What, therefore, can forty-five perfons accomplifh, when
oppofed to five hundred and thirter ?   They feel the total in-
fignificance of their fituation, and behave accordingly.   An
equal number of elbow chairs, placed once for all on the minifterial benches, would be lefs expenfive to government, and juft
about as manageable.   I call thefe, and every minifterial tool of
the fame kind, expenfive, becaufe thofe who are obliged to

B                                                    buy

*buy*, must be understood to *sell**; and those who range themselves under the banners of opposition, can only be considered, as having rated their voices too high for a purchaser in the parliamentary auction †.

There is a fashionable phrase, *the politics of the county*, which I can never hear pronounced without a glow of indignation; compared with such *politics*, even pimping is respectable. Our supreme court have, indeed, with infinite propriety, interposed to extirpate what are called in Scotland, *parchment barons*, and have thus prevented a crowd of unhappy wretches from plunging into an abyss of perjury. But, in other respects, their decision is of no consequence, since it most certainly cannot be of the smallest concern to this country, who are our electors, and representatives; or, indeed, whether we are represented at all. Our members are, most of them, the mere satellites of the minister of the day; and forward to serve his most oppressive and criminal purposes.

It seems to have been long a maxim of the monopolizing directors of our southern masters, to extirpate, as quickly as possible, every manufacture in this country, that interferes with their own. Has any body forgotten the scandalous breach of national faith, by which the Scottish distilleries have been brought to destruction? Has not the manufacture of starch also been driven, by every engine of judicial torture, to the last pang of its existence? Have not the manufacturers of paper, printed callicoes, malt liquors and glass, been harrassed by the most vexatious methods of exacting the revenue? methods equivalent to an addition of ten, or sometimes an hundred *per cent.* of the duty payable. Let us look around this insulted country, and say, on what manufacture, except the linen, government has not fastened its bloody fangs.

---

* " Damn you and your instructions too, I have BOUGHT " you, and I will SELL you," said a *worthy* representative to his constituents, when they requested him to attend to their interest in parliament. *Political Disquisitions*, vol. i. p. 280.

† To this general censure we can produce a few exceptions, but the individuals are so well known, that it would be needless to name them.

In

[ 11 ]

In the Excise annals of Scotland, that year which expired on the 5th of July 1790, produced for the duties on soap, *sixty-five thousand pounds*. On the 5th of July 1791, the annual amount of these duties was only *forty-five thousand pounds*; and by the same hopeful progress, in three years more at farthest, our ministers will enjoy the pleasure of extirpating a branch of trade, once flourishing and extensive. Two men were some years ago executed at Edinburgh for robbing the Excise Office of twenty-seven pounds; but offenders may be named, who ten thousand times better deserve the gibbet. We have seen that oppressive statutes, and a method of enforcing them, the most tyrannical, have, in a single year, deprived the revenue of twenty thousand pounds, in one line only, and have driven a crowd of industrious families out of the country; and then our legislators, to borrow the honest language of George Rous, Esq. "have the insolence to call this GOVERNMENT."

By an oriental monopoly, we have obtained the *unexampled privilege* of buying a pound of the same tea, for six or eight shillings, with which other nations would eagerly supply us for twenty-pence; nay, we have to thank our *present* illustrious minister, that this trifling vegetable has been reduced from a price still more extravagant. His popularity began by the commutation act. Wonders were promised, wonders were expected, and wonders have happened! A nation, consisting of men who call themselves *enlightened*, have consented to build up their windows, that they might enjoy the permission of sipping in the dark a cup of tea, ten *per cent.* cheaper than formerly; though not less than three hundred *per cent.* dearer than its intrinsic price.

Such are the glorious consequences of our stupid veneration for a minister, and our absurd submission to his capricious dictates!

At home Englishmen admire liberty; but abroad, they have always been harsh masters. Edward the First conquered Wales and Scotland; and at the distance of five hundred years, his name is yet remembered in both countries with traditionary horror. His actions are shaded by a degree of infamy uncommon even in the ruffian catalogue of English kings.

B 2                                              The

The rapacity of the BLACK Prince, as he has been emphatically termed, drove him out of France. At this day, there are English writers who pretend to be proud of the unprovoked massacres committed by his father and himself in that country; but on the other hand, Philip de Comines ascribes the civil wars of York and Lancaster, which followed the death of Henry the Fifth, to the indignation of divine justice.

Ireland, for many centuries, groaned under the most oppressive and absurd despotism; till, in defiance of all consequences, the immortal Swift, like another Ajax,

" *Broke the dark phalanx, and let in the light.*"

He taught his country to understand her importance. At last she resolved to assert it, and, as a necessary circumstance, she arose in arms. England saw the hazard of contending with a brave, an injured, and an indignant nation. The fabric of tyranny fell without a blow; and a short time will extinguish the last vestige of a supremacy, dishonourable and pernicious to both kingdoms.

In the East and West Indies, the conduct of Britain may be fairly contrasted with the murder of Atabaliba, and will prove equally ruinous to the detested conquerors *.

When our sublime politicians exult in the victory of Seringapatam, and the butchery of the subjects of a prince, at the dis-

---

* " The civil wars to which our violent desire of creating
" *Nabobs* gave rise, were attended with tragical events. Ben-
" gal was depopulated by every species of public distress. In
" the space of *six* years, half the great cities of this opulent
" kingdom were rendered desolate; the most fertile fields in the
" world lay waste; and FIVE MILLIONS of harmless and in-
" dustrious people were either expelled or destroyed. Want of
" foresight became more fatal than innate barbarism; and men
" found themselves wading through *blood* and *ruin*, when their
" only object was *spoil.*" *Dow's History of Indostan*, vol. iii.
p. 70. This book was published in 1772, and the present quotation refers to our conduct at that period.
In this dreadful scene, the most distinguished actor was Lord Clive. But neither four millions sterling, nor even immense quantities of opium could stifle in his bosom the agonies of reflection. In 1774, he cut his own throat.

tance of fix thoufand leagues, I am convinced from the bottom of my heart, and fo will the majority of my countrymen be, long before this century has elapfed, that it would be an event, the moft aufpicious both for Bengal and for Britain, if Cornwallis and all his myrmidons could be at once driven out of India.

But what quarter of the globe has not been convulfed by our ambition, our avarice, and our bafenefs? The tribes of the Pacific ocean are polluted by the moft loathfome of difeafes; our brandy has brutalized or extirpated the Indians of the weftern continent; and we have hired by thoufands the wretched furvivors to the tafk of bloodfhed. On the fhores of Africa, we bribe whole nations by drunkennefs, to robbery and murder; while in the face of earth and heaven, our fenators affemble to fanctify the practice.

Our North American colonies were eftablifhed, defended, and loft, by a fucceffion of long and bloody wars, and at a recorded expence of at leaft two or three hundred millions fterling *. We ftill retain Canada, at an annual charge of fix or feven hundred thoufand pounds. This fum is wrefted from us by an excife, which revels in the deftruction of manufactures, and the beggary of ten thoufand honeft families †. From the province itfelf we never raifed, nor hope to raife, a fhilling of revenue; and the fole reafon why its inhabitants endure our dominion for a month longer is, to fecure the money we fpend among them.

---

* In the war of 1775, Britifh officers pilfered books from a public library, which had been founded at Philadelphia by an individual more truly eftimable than many of the whole profeffion put together; I need hardly fubjoin the name of Franklin.

† Look into Kearfely's or Robertfon's tax-tables: What concife! what tremenduous volumes! When our political writers boaft of Britifh liberty, they remind us of Smollet's cobler in Bedlam bombarding Conftantinople. If the victims who groan under our yoke, were acquainted with the confufion and flavery which our avarice or mad ambition have inflicted on ourfelves, a very confiderable fhare of their abhorrence would be converted into contempt or pity.

CHAP.

# CHAP II.

'Tis time to take enormity by the forehead and brand it,
BEN JOHNSON.

" DURING the reigns of Charles and James the Second,
" above sixty thousand Nonconformists suffered, of
" whom *five thousand* DIED IN PRISON. On a moderate com-
" putation, these persons were pillaged of FOURTEEN MILLI-
" ONS of property. Such was the tolerating, liberal, candid
" spirit of the Church of England *." This estimate cannot
be intended to include Scotland, for it is likely that here alone,
Episcopacy sacrificed sixty thousand victims. Of all sorts of follies, the records of the Church form the most outrageous bur-
lesque on the human understanding. As to Charles the Second,
it is full time that we should be spared from the hereditary in-
sult of a holiday, for what Lord Gardenstone has justly termed
" his BANEFUL RESTORATION."
It is vulgarly understood that our political millenium commenced with " the *glorious* Revolution." Let the reader judge
from what follows.
" Two hundred thousand pounds a year *bestowed upon the*
" *parliament*, have already (1693) drawn out of the pockets
" of the subjects MORE MONEY than *all our kings since the Con-*
" *quest have had from the nation!*—The King (William) has
" about six score members, whom I can reckon, who are in
" places, and are thereby so entirely at his devotion, that though
" they have mortal feuds, *when out of the House*, and though
" they are violently of opposite parties, in their notions of go-
" vernment, yet they vote as lumpingly as *the lawn sleeves*.
" The House is so *officered* by those who have places and pen-

---

* *Vide* Flower on the French Constitution, p. 437, and his
Authorities.

" sions,

" fions, that the King can baffle any bill, quafh all grievances,
" and ftifle all accompts *."

A pawnbroker defcending from the pillory would not be
fuffered to refume his profeffion. A porter convicted of theft,
would be deprived of his ticket. We might be tempted to ima-
gine, that a folicitude to embrace pollution, can hardly exift
even in the meaneft and moft worthlefs rank of mankind. It
feems incredible, that an affembly confifting of *Gentlemen*, fhall
firft by a folemn vote difcharge one of their members as *a raf-
cal*, and in a fhort time after, *place him at their head.* That fuch
a cafe has actually happened, appears upon record.

In the year 1711, the Houfe of Commons refolved, " That
" *Robert Walpole, Efquire,* having been this feffion of parlia-
" liament committed a prifoner to the Tower, and expelled this
" Houfe for *a breach of truft* in the execution of his office, and
" NOTORIOUS CORRUPTION, when Secretary at War, was,
" and is incapable of being elected a member to ferve in this
" prefent parliament." Such an expulfion would for ever have
bolted him out of any fociety but a Britifh fenate. In 1715,
when a new parliament was called, he refumed his feat. He
rofe fuperior to competition ; and the end of his career was
worthy of his outfet. Yet his character can lofe nothing by a
comparifon with that of his conftituents, the burgeffes of Lynn,
who attempted inftantly upon his expulfion, to return him a fecond time as their reprefentative, but their choice was rejected.
Nor was it becaufe Walpole had pilfered five hundred guineas
that he was expelled and fent to the Tower. He was a *Whig,*
and at that time the majority in the Houfe of Commons were
*Tories.* This was regarded as the true caufe of his fentence †.

---

* Burgh's Political Difquifitions, vol. 1, p. 405.

† George the Second, on his acceffion, had refolved to dif-
mifs Walpole. The minifter offered on condition of keeping his
place, to obtain an addition of an hundred thoufand pounds *per
annum* to the civil lift, and a jointure of an hundred thoufand
pounds to Queen Caroline. His terms were accepted. It is
impoffible for the human mind to conceive a more fordid tranf-
action. Edmund Burke, in what he calls an appeal to the old
whigs, has gravely affured us, that " Walpole was an *honour-
" able* man, and a *found* WHIG. He was not a prodigal and cor-
" rupt minifter. He was far from governing by *corruption*."

The

The Earl of Wharton, *another* WHIG, was fined in a thousand pounds for an outrage too grofs to be repeated. This did not deprive him of his feat in the House of Peers, nor impede his progrefs to the government of Ireland, where his conduct rivalled that of Rumbold in Bengal, or Verres in Sicily.—About the year 1770, General Burgoyne was fined in a thousand pounds for bribery at an election for Prefton. He enjoys a feat in the prefent p—liament.

On the fubject of parliamentary corruption, no writer has fpoken with more franknefs and perfpicuity, than Mr. Dodding-ton, in his celebrated Diary. In a converfation with the Duke of Newcaftle, in 1753, about an election for Bridgewater, there is the following curious paffage : " I recommended my two " parfons, Burroughs and Franklin. The Duke entered into " it very cordially, and anfwered me, that they fhould have " the firft crown livings that fhould be vacant in their parts, if " we would look out and fend him the firft intelligence." And again, "Mr. Pelham declared, that I had a good deal of " *marketable ware*, PARLIAMENTARY INTEREST, and that if " I would empower him to offer it all to the King, *without* " *conditions*, he would be anfwerable to bring the affair to a good " account.—The Duke of Newcaftle faid, that what I did was " *very great*, that he often thought with furprife, at the cafe " and *cheapnefs* of the election at Weymouth, *that they had* " NOTHING *like it*. I faid, I believed there were few who " could give his Majefty fix members for *nothing*.—The elec- " tion coft me three thoufand four hundred pounds. I was " fairly chofen, nor would the returning officer have dared not " to return me, had : not been encouraged by the fervants of " adminiftration. The borough was loft, and loft folely by a " Lord of the Bed-chamber, and the Cuftom-houfe Officers." *(Par nobile fratrum!)* " Lord Bute had told Anfon, that " room muft be made for Lord Parker ; who replied, that all " was engaged. Bute faid, *What, my Lord, the King's Admi-* " *ralty boroughs full, and the King not acquainted with it!* An- " fon feemed quite difconcerted, and knew not what to fay *."

* Doddington's Diary, 3d ed. p. 256, 283, 293, 309, *et feq.*
This

This agrees exactly with the account given by Mr. Courtney, in a late debate in the House of Commons, where he observed, that members came into parliament with a label at their mouths, inscribed, *Yes*, or *No*. The state of British representation has been often examined and censured. A few particulars may serve as a specimen of the rest.

England is said to contain eight millions of inhabitants, who send to the House of Commons five hundred and thirteen members. At this rate, every million ought, upon an average, to chuse sixty-four representatives. The cities of London and Westminster contain between them, about a million of people, who elect not *sixty-four*, but *six* members for parliament. The borough of Old Sarum, which contains only *one* inhabitant, sends *two* members.

On this topick, a short extract from Mr. Burgh's Political Disquisitions, may entertain the reader.—" Two hundred and " fifty-four members are elected by five thousand seven hundred " and twenty-three votes; now, the most numerous meeting of " the Commons ever known, was on occasion of the debate " about Walpole, A. D. 1741. There were then five hundred " and two in the House. Therefore, two hundred and fifty- " four comes very near a majority of the House, or the *whole* " *acting* and *efficient* number. And the greatest part of these " illustrious five thousand seven hundred and twenty-three, " who have the power of constituting lawgivers over the pro- " perty of the nation, are themselves persons of no property *."

The writer has here committed a slight inaccuracy; for, in the debate about Walpole, these two hundred and fifty-four members, who are not, in fact, elected by a two hundredth part of the nation, would have seemed an actual majority of six votes against the whole other representatives in the House. In the year 1770, the English nation became jealous that their liberties were in danger, because Government had interfered in the election of Mr. Wilkes, as a member for the county of Middlesex. The letters of Junius are chiefly employed upon this

* Political Disquisitions, vol. 1, p. 45.

C

topic. Junius, with all his merit, refembled a barber, who plucks out a fingle hair, when he ought to be fharing your beard. It could not be of the leaft confequence to the county of Middlefex, nor is it of any concern to any other county in England, who are their reprefentatives, fince the two hundred and fifty-four members who are elected by A TWO HUN-DREDTH PART of the nation, and the forty-five make-weight Scotch members, are alone fufficient to infure a majority. The fubject is too abfurd to admit of an argument, and too deteftable for declamation. If Government were candidly to fend two hundred and fifty-four excifemen, or clerks from the Bank of England, into parliament, in place of thefe two hundred and fifty-four members, it would fave the expence of election, and a great part of the neceffary expence of corruption. It is true, that the mafters of rotten boroughs are often inrolled in the ranks of oppofition ; and among others, the Earl of Chatham, began his progrefs as a member for Old Sarum. But an oppofition always confifts, in part, of adventures, who, as Dr. Johnfon obferves, " having eftimated themfelves at two high a price, " are only angry that they are not *bought* \*." There is a cant expreffion in this country, that our Government is defervedly *the wonder and envy of the world.* With better reafon it may be faid, that Parliament is a mere outwork of the court, a phalanx of mercenaries embattled againft the reafon, the happinefs, and the liberty of mankind. The game laws, the dog act, the fhop tax, the window tax, the pedlars tax, the attorney tax, and a thoufand others, give us a right to wifh that their authors had been hanged.

---

\* *Vide* Falfe Alarm.

CHAP.

———————————————Felicior effem
Angustis opibus: mallem tolerare Sabinos,
Et Vejos: brevior duxi securius ævum.
Ipsa nocet moles.                               CLAUDIAN.

IT is now eighty-eight years since * we surprised Gibraltar.
We have retained this barren, useless rock, under the pretence of protecting our trade in the Mediterranean; and it is
even a sorry conceit in Britain that we are thus masters of a kind
of toll-bar to the entrance of that sea. Had the passage been
only five hundred yards wide, this fancy would have had some
foundation. But, unfortunately, the *Strait*, as we call it, is
*twenty miles* in breadth; so that all the ships in the world may
pass it every day, in contempt of all our batteries. As to the
protection of our merchants, it is equally superfluous, for our
commerce to that part of Europe was far more extensive, long
before we possessed Gibraltar, than it is at this moment †; and
this unquestionable fact proves the absolute impertinence of the
whole scheme. A plain comparison from domestic life will il-
lustrate what I say. Let us put the case, that a private gentle-
man is like Britain, overwhelmed with debt. He builds and
furnishes a handsome inn on the road to his country seat; and
he gives the premises to his butler, with a pension of five hundred pounds, on condition, that in dirty weather, he shall be
suffered to pull off his boots in the kitchen. But were even the
port of Gibraltar sunk to the centre of the earth, we can have
no want of shelter at the shortest distance. There are three
ports on the opposite side of the Strait. Besides, we cannot retain this fortress, unless we preserve a superiority at sea, and as

* In 1704.
† This circumstance has been fully explained by Dr. Adam
Smith, in his Inquiry, book 4, chap. 7.

long as we preferve that fuperiority, Gibraltar is of no confequence. For the memorable progrefs of Admiral Blake on the
coaft of Barbary proves, that while we can launch a victorious
navy, manned as it is by a race of veterans beyond all praife,
we can always command a free navigation in every harbour of
the globe. So much for the importance of this boafted acquifition. Let us now confider its expence ; and on this head the
reader may, if he thinks proper, prepare himfelf for aftonifh-
ment. The fortrefs, for a long period paft, has coft us five hundred thoufand pounds a year, befides the extraordinary advances
in time of war, and the fums which the garrifon, by fober induftry, might have earned at home in time of peace. For the
fake of moderation, let us compute that Gibraltar, during the
whole fpace of our poffeffion, has required, upon an average,
only two hundred thoufand pounds *per annum ;* on multiplying
this fum by eighty-eight, we are prefented with an amount of
feventeen millions and fix hundred thoufand pounds fterling.
Could the premifes be difputed, the total expence would ex-
ceed credibility ; for at the rate of five *per cent.* of compound
intereft, a fum doubles itfelf in fourteen years ; and, confe-
quently, in the courfe of eighty-four years, from 1704, to 1788,
the firft payment of two hundred thoufand pounds will increafe
to twelve millions and eight hundred thoufand. The fimple
intereft of this fum, for the four additional years, from 1788 to
1792 inclufive, amounts to two millions five hundred and fixty
thoufand pounds, and the whole arifes to *fifteen millions three
hundred and fixty thoufand pounds.* This, however, concerns
only *one* year of our conqueft. The firft four years extend in
the whole to *fifty-feven millions and fix hundred thoufand pounds
fterling.* Another lofs alfo muft be taken into this unfathom-
able accompt. The garrifon of this fortrefs confifts always of
at leaft four thoufand men, and fometimes of more than twice
that number. An ordinary workman can earn ten fhillings a
week, and the labour of four thoufand fuch workmen is worth
to the public above an hundred thoufand pounds *per annum.*
This adds one third part more of additional lofs. The total
expence therefore, which this acquifition exhaufted in the firft

four

four years only, including the legal intereſt of our money down to this day, cannot have been leſs than *eighty-ſix millions four hundred thouſand pounds*. We are likewiſe entitled to compute not only what we have poſitively loſt, but what we might with equal certainty have gained. Britain and Ireland contain about an hundred and four thouſand ſquare miles, and if this ſum of eighty-ſix millions four hundred thouſand pounds had been expended on the purpoſes of agriculture, it would have ſupplied a fund of eight hundred and thirty pounds ſterling for every ſquare mile. Hence, inſtead of an intereſt of *five* per cent. the funds thus employed would have returned a profit of *ten* or *twenty*, or perhaps of *fifty* per cent.

The reader may proſecute, and contemplate the ſequel of this calculation. All the current caſh in Europe, or in the world, would come infinitely ſhort of diſcharging ſuch a reckoning. Britain may be ſuppoſed at this time to contain about fifteen hundred thouſand families, beſides thoſe who are ſupported upon charity. Now, dividing the preſent annual expence of five hundred thouſand pounds equally among them, it amounts to a ſhare of ſix ſhillings and eight pence *per* family. The money ought to be raiſed under a diſtinct title, ſuch as the Gibraltar *additional ſhilling of land tax*, the Gibraltar *malt tax*, the Gibraltar *exciſe on tobacco*, the Gibraltar *game licence*, the Gibraltar *horſe licence*, the Gibraltar *attorney licence*, or the Gibraltar *ſtamp duty on legacies*. In that caſe, the nation would inſtantly conſider what they are about, and caſt off ſuch a prepoſterous burden. The payment of ſix ſhillings and eight pence is frequently the ſmalleſt part of the grievance. By the expence of exciſemen, of proſecutions, and of penalties, five ſhillings of revenue may often coſt a Britiſh *freeman* ten times as many pounds ſterling *.

Before

---

* I ſhall mention an example in point, which occurs while I am now writing. An old woman had been in the practice of ſupplying her neighbours with halfpennyworths of ſnuff. She was ordered, under a penalty of *fifty pounds*, to pay *five ſhillings* for a licence, and ſhe did ſo. Had ſhe been able to buy from the manufacturer four pounds of ſnuff at a time, the buſineſs might

Before the acquisition of Gibraltar, England, in the whole course of her history, had only three wars with Spain. The first in 1588, was produced by the piracies of Drake and others, and by the assistance which Elizabeth afforded to the Dutch revolters. The second war was likewise unprovoked on the part of Spain. Cromwell found it necessary to vent the turbulence of his subjects in a foreign quarrel, and Jamaica was invaded and seized without even a pretence of justice. On this conquest chiefly has England founded that hopeful branch of her commerce, the Slave-Trade, while the climate has annually extirpated, by thousands, the vagrants from Europe. The third Spanish war had an origin worthy of its predecessors. The King of Spain, by his will, transferred his dominions to a Prince of the house of Bourbon. His subjects consented or submitted to the choice, and England, with a degree of insolence unmatched in history, interfered in favour of an Austrian candidate. The contest ended with our acquisition of Minorca, nd Gibraltar; an injury to Spain of the most offensive nature. Since that period her court has always been forward to contend with us; and five wars*, begun and terminated in the short space of sixty-five years, assures us of their indelible indignation. Nor can we be surprised at their animosity; for what would an Englishman say or feel, were Plymouth and Dover fortified by a French garrison? Happily for the species, our countrymen at Gibraltar have been but seldom attacked. Hence, in a time of war, they have commonly inflicted and suffered far less mischief than must have been committed on both sides in a piratical ex-

---

might have rested there; but as this was beyond her power, it was required by the terriers of taxation, that she should make oath, once a year, to the quantity she sold. Her memory failed, and she is now, with a crowd of other victims, in an excise court, which will very possibly bring her to beggary. This is like a drop in the ocean of excise. The very sound of the word announces utter destruction; for it is derived from a Latin verb, which signifies *to cut up by the roots.*
What " our most excellent constitution" may be in theory, I neither know nor care. In practice, it is altogether a CONSPIRACY OF THE RICH AGAINST THE POOR.
* *Viz.* in 1718, in 1727, in 1739, in 1762, and in 1779.

pedition

pedition to the coaft of Peru, in defolating the plains of Hin-
doftan, in burning the fhipping at St. Maloes, or in ftorming the
peftilential ramparts of the Havannah *.

In 1708, we captured Minorca, and after what has been
faid as to Gibraltar, it is unneceffary to expatiate on the mon-
fterous expences which it muft have coft us during half a century, till it was in 1756 furrendered to the French. On this
event the whole Englifh nation feemed to have run out of their
fenfes. Yet to the lofs of this fortrefs, we may in fome meafure attribute our *fuccefs*, as it was called, in that war; for the
charge of fupporting Minorca muft have been felt as a dead
weight upon our other operations. It was reftored in 1763, and
in 1781, it was a fecond time, and I hope for ever, feparated
from the Britifh dominions. By the lofs of this fortrefs we
fave an inceffant and extravagant expence. With me it is an
object of regret, that the brave Elliot and his garrifon had not
been forced to capitulate by the firft bomb difcharged againft
them. The individuals, acting as they did, from the moft generous and honourable principles, have acquired and deferved
our warmeft gratitude; and, as it may be expected that fuch
events will hereafter become lefs frequent, their glory will de-
fcend with increafing luftre to the laft generations of mankind.
But their efforts were fatal to this country; for it is felf-evident
that we had much better have wanted this mock appendage of
empire. The fiege itfelf produced fcenes of fuch ftupenduous
deftruction, that they cannot be perufed without horror. Nine
years of peace have fince elapfed, and, in that time, including
the endlefs expence of fortifications, it is probable that Gibraltar has coft us at leaft five millions fterling; befides, we have
been again on the verge of a war with Spain, which has added
a comfortable *item* of four millions to the debts of the nation.
If the annual expence of Gibraltar amounts to five hundred
thoufand pounds, this is about one thirty-fecond part of our

---

* The Major of a Britifh regiment who ferved at that fiege,
had in his company, on his arrival at Cuba, an hundred and nine
healthy men. Of thefe, as he himfelf told me, *five* only returned to Europe.

public

public revenue. Nothing but the power of its difposal can obtain for a Britifh minifter a majority in the Houfe of Commons.
Three hundred and twenty members are about the ufual number *under his influence* \*; and therefore the patronage of Gibraltar may be conjectured to purchafe ten votes in the market
of St. Stephen's chapel +.

Though writers have prefumed to fpecify the annual charge
of Gibraltar, an exact eftimate cannot poffibly be obtained.
The public accounts are prefented to parliament in a ftate of in-
extricable confufion. Indeed, their immenfe bulk would alone
be fufficient to place them far beyond the reach of any human
comprehenfion. A fingle circumftance may ferve to fhow the
way in which parliamentary bufinefs is commonly performed.
A ftatute was paffed and printed fome years ago, containing
three fucceffive references to the *thirty-*FIRST day of November.

For a foreign conteft, our government is moft wretchedly
adapted. In the war of 1756, Frederick, that Shakefpeare of
kings, fought and conquered five different nations. In the
courfe of his miraculous campaigns, he neither added a fingle
impoft, nor attempted to borrow a fingle fhilling. At the fame
time our boafted Earl of Chatham was overwhelming this country with taxes, and contracting an annual debt of fifteen or
twenty millions fterling. With a more deftructive minifter no
nation was ever curfed. Yet this man we prefer to Sir Robert
Walpole, a ftatefman, whofe maxim it was to keep us, if poffible, at peace with all the world.

In 1662, Dunkirk, then poffeffed by England, coft an annual

---

\* When the whole ftrength of each party is called forth, a
minority are commonly within an hundred voices of the minifter,
which correfponds with tolerable accuracy to the computation in
the text. In the regency queftion, Mr. Pitt, with the whole
nation at his back, muftered only two hundred and fixty-nine
members.

+ In the Spanifh negociation in 1757, the Earl of Chatham
(then Mr. Pitt) propofed to cede Gibraltar to Spain, and again,
in 1761, he offered it as *the price of the Family Compact.* Vide
*His Life,* in two large volumes juft publifhed. This propofal
evinces, that the fortrefs was not, in Mr. Pitt's opinion, of much
importance to Britain.

expence

expence of an hundred and twenty thoufand pounds. At the fame period the whole revenues of the nation did not amount to eleven hundred thoufand pounds. The retention of the town muft have proved a hot-bed of future wars with France. Charles the Second, at this time fold it to Lewis the Fourteenth, for the fum of four hundred thoufand pounds. This was, I believe, the only wife, laudable, or even innocent action of his reign. It had almoft produced a rebellion ; and, as Mr. Hume obferves, " has " not had the good fortune, to be juftified by any party."

Domeftic improvement is, in all cafes, more advantageous than military acquifition. Yet in the great outlines of our hiftory, we have inceffantly forfaken the former; to purfue the latter. James the Firft, though in private, and even in public life, univerfally defpifed, was one of the beft fovereigns that ever fat on the Britifh throne. Without a fingle quality which could recommend him to our efteem, he preferved the Englifh nation, though much againft their will, in peace, during his entire reign of twenty-two years. Hence both iflands made rapid advances in wealth and profperity. " Never," fays Stowe, " was there any people, lefs confiderate, and lefs thank- " ful than at this time, *being not willing to endure the memory of* " *their prefent happinefs.*" On the fame principles of rapine, which dictated the retention of Dunkirk, James has been feverely blamed for delivering back to the Dutch three of their fortified towns, which had been put into the poffeffion of Elizabeth. Mr. Hume has, with much propriety, indicated his conduct. Had it been poffible that the life of fuch a prince, and the tranquillity of this country, could have been prolonged to the prefent day, it is beyond the power of Britifh vanity to conceive the accumulated progrefs of Britifh opulence. Both iflands would, long before this time, have advanced to a ftate of cultivation, not inferior to that of China. The productions of the foil, and the number of inhabitants, might have exceeded, by tenfold, their prefent amount. Public roads, canals, bridges, and buildings of every defcription, muft have multiplied far beyond what our moft fanguine wifhes are capable of conceiving. A fhort review of the deftruction committed by foreign wars within the laft hundred

D                                                              years

years of our hiſtory, can hardly fail to amuſe, and may perhaps inſtruct the reader.

## CHAP. IV.

*Facilis eſt deſcenſus Averni.*         **Virg.**

'Tis eaſy into hell to fall;
But to get out again is all.

" THE ground of the firſt war," ſays Dr. Swift, " after " the Revolution, as to the part we had in it, was to " make France acknowledge the late king, and to recover *Hud-* " *ſon's Bay.* But during that whole war the ſea was almoſt " entirely neglected, and the greateſt part of ſix millions *annu-* " *ally*, employed *to enlarge the frontier of the Dutch.* For the " king was a general, but not an admiral; and although king " of England, was a native of Holland.

" After ten years of fighting, to little purpoſe, after the loſs " of above *an hundred thouſand men*, and a debt remaining of " *twenty millions*, we at length hearkened to the terms of " Peace, which was concluded with great advantages to the " Empire and Holland, but *none at all to us \*.*"

This account does not give us much encouragement to ſend for a ſecond ſovereign from Holland. Dutch generoſity appears to have proved a very miſerable bargain. It is hardly poſſible that James, with all his prieſts and dragoons, could have committed one hundredth part of this havock. So much for a Proteſtant hero, and a glorious Revolution.

William aſcended and ſupported his throne by a ſeries of the meaneſt and moſt diſgraceful expedients. He excited Argyle and Monmouth to rebellion. He bribed the ſervants of James to betray to himſelf the ſecrets of their maſter. He inſtructed

---

\* The Conduct of the Allies.

theſe

thefe minifters to drive the King of England into thofe very
meafures which forced a Revolution. He was bafe enough to
deny the ligitimacy of the Prince of Wales; he taught two
thanklefs daughters to forfake, and ruin, and infult their father.
When embarking for this country, " he took Heaven to wit-
" nefs, that he had not the leaft intention to invade or fubdue
" the kingdom of England, much lefs to make himfelf mafter
" thereof, or to invert or prejudice the lawful fucceffion *."
James had quarreiled with the Church of England, and this was
one of the chief c . .es of his deftruction. Yet all the bifhops,
except eight, as well as many temporal peers, refufed to take
the oaths to the new government; and Sancroft, Archbifhop of
Canterbury, who had been at the head of the oppofition to
James, was, along with five other bifhops, depofed for his re-
fufal. The convention parliament who made William King of
England, were *elected by himfelf,* and contained, befides other
extraordinary materials, *fifty members of the Common Council of
London.* With this very parliament he was immediately on the
worft terms; and Sutherland, Marlborough, and Admiral Ruffel, with many other chiefs of his party, entered into a confpiracy for his expulfion. The Irifh rebels had forfeited lands to
the value of three millions three hundred and twenty thoufand
pounds. This immenfe property William divided almoft altogether among his Dutch favourites, and the Countefs of Orkney, an Englifh concubine, whofe fervices were rewarded with
an eftate of twenty-fix thoufand pounds a year; while, at the
fame time, with the moft fordid ingratitude, he turned his back
on the family of Monmouth, who had been his tool and his vic-
tim. Thefe acts of robbery were reverfed by parliament. I
pafs over the tragedies of Glencoe and Darien, for on fuch a
character, they reflect no peculiar reproach. William was the
father of our public debt, which he multiplied as much as poffible,. that befides other mean purpofes, he might attach to his
perfonal fafety the creditors of the nation. As to parliament,
in 1690, the Speaker " promifed to the king to manage his

---

* Macpherfon's Hiftory of Britain, vol. 1, chap. 8.

" own

" own party, *provided he might be furnished with money to pur-*
" *chafe votes *.*" His majefty confented. In the progrefs of
this confpiracy, his agent was expelled from the Houfe of Commons, for accepting from the City of London a bribe of a
thoufand guineas. A bribe of ten thoufand pounds, from the
Eaft-India Company, " was traced to the king † ;" a magiftrate,
whofe office it was to fign the warrant for executing a pick-
pocket, William extinguifhed this inquiry by a prorogation,
" Thus ended," fays the hiftorian, " *a wretched farce,* in which
" the feeble efforts for obtaining juftice were fcarce lefs dif-
" graceful than venality itfelf." On the 20th December 1697,
the Commons granted William feven hundred thoufand pounds
a year for the fupport of the civil lift. This comprehended
fifty thoufand pounds a year, which he promifed to pay to
King James's queen as her jointure, and fifty thoufand pounds
a year, which he demanded as neceffary to eftablifh the houfehold of the Duke of Gloucefter. To the queen he never paid
a farthing, and to the Duke only fifteen thoufand pounds a
year. This prince died on the 24th of July 1700, and in 1701
the Commons, after a violent debate with the adherents of the
court, compelled William to refund the fifty thoufand pounds,
which he had engaged to pay to the exiled queen ; and above
twenty thoufand pounds, which the Duke of Gloucefter had
left behind him ‡. Mr. Pitt complains of authors who publifh

---

\* Macpherfon's Hiftory of Great Britain, vol. 1, chap. 10,
† Ibid. vol. 2, chap. 2.
‡ Macpherfon, vol. ii. chap. 3 and 4. The hiftorian has re-
lated this anecdote in fuch a manner, that we cannot learn what
fums the exiled queen ought to have received. When her jointure is twice mentioned in chapter 3, he calls it fifty thoufand
pounds a year. But after four years, in chapter 4, he contra-
dicts this ftatement, by informing us, that William had retained
*the* fifty thoufand pounds due to her, which, with the reverfion
by the death of the Duke of Gloucefter, amounted to " *near* an
" hundred thoufand pounds." By the account in chapter 3,
the whole fums, including intereft, fhould have been about two
hundred and fifty thoufand pounds.
This miftake is hardly worth notice here, but is mentioned
merely to fhew that one may fometimes be forced to feek a
way through very difcordant materials.

libel

libels on the Revolution. To forbid a person from publishing
his sentiments on a historical event which happened above an
hundred years ago, is in itself an example of the utmost infolence of despotism. To depose one tyrant was highly proper ;
but it was not less foolish to exalt another *.

*More cost more honour,* says the proverb ; and by this rule the
Revolution was certainly a more splendid transaction than the
nation had ever seen. " The expences of England, from the
" landing of the Prince of Orange on the 5th of November
" 1688, to the 29th of September 1691, had amounted to near
" EIGHTEEN MILLIONS. Besides, great arrears were owing
" to the army in Ireland, the navy was *destitute of stores*, and *the
" ships were out of repair* †." In 1693, a bill passed both
Houses, providing for annual sessions of parliament, and a new
election once in three years. To this bill, the FOUNDER OF
ENGLISH FREEDOM refused his assent, which in 1694 was obtained by compulsion. After having told all the world for ten
years, that James had imposed a spurious prince upon the nation, he engaged in 1697, to obtain that prince to be declared
his successor ‡. A man of common spirit would rather have
been a chimney sweeper than such a sovereign.

As for the inferior actors in the Revolution, we may inquire
*what have they done ?* They did not transfer the load of taxes
from the poor to the rich. They did not extirpate entails, and

---

* Smollet's character of William is a curious jumble.
" He was religious, temperate, *generally just* and *sincere.*—He
" involved these kingdoms in foreign connections, which, in all
" probability, will be *productive of their ruin.* He scrupled not
" to employ *all the engines of corruption.* He entailed upon the
" nation a growing debt, and a system of politics big with
" misery, despair, and destruction." The rest of this passage is
too long for insertion ; but the author's inference appears to be,
that William was the most ruinous sovereign who ever sat on
the throne of England.
† Macpherson, vol. ii. chap. 1. All our continental wars and
subsidies, from 1688, to this day, must be ascribed to the Revolution.
‡ Ibid. vol. ii. chap. 3. The author adds, " The succes-
" sors provided by the act of settlement, he either *despised* or
" *abhorred.*" These were the illustrious House of Brunswick.

rotten

rotten boroughs. They did not eſtabliſh an univerſal right of conſcience, and an univerſal right of citizenſhip. They did not advance even a ſingle ſtep towards exalting the motely parliament of England into the actual repreſentatives of a free people. They did not avoid a moſt deſtructive and endleſs quarrel on the continent. They did not reduce the civil liſt even to the prodigal eſtabliſhment of Charles the Second *. They did not extirpate the moſt abſurd and extravagant prerogatives of the ſovereign, to adjourn or diſſolve a parliament at pleaſure, to baſtardize a peerage with the puppets of deſpotiſm, to interpoſe a refuſal to the moſt neceſſary laws, and to plunge at his will three nations into blood and bankruptcy. *What then did they do ?* 'They obtained for their countrymen a right *to petition* THE CROWN †. They ſettled the ſucceſſion on a family whom their hero, for what reaſon he beſt knew, *deſpiſed* and *abhorred.* The whole work was a change, not of meaſures, but of maſters. Where then ſtands the difference between the trimmer Halifax, and the trimmer Thurlow ; between Sutherland the traitor to all parties, and our Hibernian panegyriſt of the Baſtile ? The Duke of

---

* *Viz.* Four hundred and ſixty thouſand pounds. The ſettlement of ſeven hundred thouſand pounds is no doubt one of thoſe *wiſe* and *wholeſome* PROVISIONS ſo gratefully referred to in Mr. Pitt's late proclamation. There can be no queſtion, that in the courſe of an hundred years, the civil liſt has reduced many hundred thouſands of his Majeſty's " *faithful* and *loving* ſub-" jects" to beggary. That *the weakeſt come always to the worſt,* is a trite obſervation. The principal hardſhips of every tax muſt in the laſt reſort fall upon the poor. At this day the *civil liſt,* with all its abyſs of appendages, abſorbes above eleven hundred thouſand pounds *per annum* of Engliſh money. This expence would, at leaſt in Scotland, be more than ſufficient to maintain two hundred and fifty thouſand paupers, for thoſe in the poor's houſe of the pariſh of St. Cuthbert's, near Edinburgh, coſt but about four pounds each *per annum.*
    Hence it follows, that the royal eſtabliſhment is in fact equal to an eſtabliſhment of many myriads of beggars. As to the ELECTORAL HOARD, we have curious and authentic information, but this ſubject deſerves a chapter by itſelf.
    † They might as well have ſpoke about the right of blowing one's noſe. Yet this miſerable ſtipulation, extracted from the very dregs of ſlavery, has been thought of infinite conſeqvence.

Marlborough

Marlborough gave a juſt account both of the Whigs and Tories, "I do not believe," ſaid he, "that either party is ſwayed by "any true principles of conſcience or honeſty. Their profeſ-"ſions are always different; their views preciſely the ſame. "They both graſp at the poſſeſſion of power; and the Prince "who gives them the moſt is their greateſt favourite *." Were farther evidence wanting, Burnet, himſelf both a whig and a courtier, tells us that the whigs *ſet every thing to ſale*. He complained of the practice of bribing parliament to the king, and William aſſured him, *that it was not poſſible to help it*.

As a partial defence of our anceſtors it may be urged, that in the end of the laſt century, the nation was unripe for a rational conſtitution. But ſince we know this to be true, why are we diſturbed with rhapſodies on one of the moſt queſtionable combinations that ever deformed hiſtory ? Does any body compare the packed convention parliaments of the two kingdoms, in 1689, with the democratical members of the firſt national aſſembly of France ? As well might we parallel Charles Jenkinſon with the Duke of Sully, or the aſſaſſin of Culloden with the conqueror at Bannockburn. Did the philoſophical and conciſe decrees of the French patriots grovel in the feudal jargon of ſubjecting a people and their poſterity forever to the aſſignees of a Dutchman who was univerſally deteſted ? As well might we fancy a reſemblance between the daubing of a ſign-poſt, and the pencil of Reynolds, or the exerciſe of a ſchool-boy and the ſtanzas of Buchanan.

Upon the whole, as William betrayed James into ſeveral of thoſe crimes by which a revolution became neceſſary, his memory is an object not of reſpect but abhorrence. His conduct was like that of an incendiary who firſt ſets fire to your houſe, and then claims ten times the worth of the whole building for his ſervice in quenching it. To praiſe him and his revolution, diſcovers an ignorance of hiſtory, or a contempt of common honeſty. It is as much a burleſque upon reaſon, as when a King of England calls himſelf King of France ; or as when a

---

* Macpherſon, vol. ii. chap. 8.

person, like Henry the Eighth, whose word is trusted by nobody, assumes for his title *Defender of the Faith.*

But since the authors of the revolution did not surpass the diminutive standard of Court integrity, why has our temple of venality * for so long a time resounded with the wretched larum of whig families and whig virtues ? Why should common men wander from their natural and just progress to obscurity, and mock the attention of future ages ? Had Archimedes been only the best archer at the siege of Syracuse, had Columbus lived and died but the most expert pilot in the port of Genoa, had the eloquence of Shakespeare shrunk to a level with the dramatick mushrooms of this day, these memorable benefactors of mankind had vanished into instant oblivion. Had Thomas Paine been nothing superior to a vagabond seamen, a bankrupt staymaker, a discarded exciseman, a porter in the streets of Philadelphi, or whatever else the insanity of Grub-street chuses to call him, an hundred thousand copies of his writings had never announced his name in every village on the globe, where the English language is spoken, nor would the rays of royal indignation have illuminated that character which they cannot scorch.

---

## CHAP. V.

*Nulla unquam de morte hominis cunctatio longa est.*

No delay as to the death of a man is ever too long.    JUVENAL.

IN the war which ended by the peace of Ryswick, seven hundred millions sterling were spent, and eight hundred thousand men perished, yet none of the parties gained one penny of

---

* In the Anecdotes of Lord Chatham, we are told that Mr. Pelham was intrusted with *what is usally called* THE POCKET LIST OF THE HOUSE OF COMMONS ; and Mr. Pitt sometimes said to his friends, " I was obliged to BORROW the Duke of Newcastle's " *majority,* to carry on the public business."

money,

money, or almoſt one foot of territory. In 1693, Lewis made very ample offers for peace which William refuſed. Had William accepted theſe offers of Lewis, " the war of the firſt grand " alliance would have ended *four years ſooner than it did*, and the " war of the ſecond grand alliance *might have been prevented* \*. " During ſome years previous to the peace of Ryſwick, the " price of corn in England was *double*, and in Scotland *qua-* " *druple* its ordinary rate ; and in one of thoſe years, it was be- " lieved that in Scotland *eighty thouſand people died of want* †."

The war which followed the Revolution coſt England *ſixty millions ſterling* ‡. Let us ſuppoſe that an equal ſhare of this ſum was ſpent in each of the nine years, during which it laſted, and at ſix *per cent.* the compound intereſt of the ſums advanced annually up to the peace of Ryſwick in 1697, amounts to *fifteen millions ſterling*. Four thouſand merchantmen were taken by the enemy §; and De-Foe, in one of his pamplets, tells us, that the damage in this way had been computed at twenty millions. The intereſt of this ſum, eſtimated in the ſame manner with that of the public expences up to the peace, will produce five millions. But that our calculations may be perfectly ſafe, let us bring down both principal and intereſt to *fifteen millions*, and we ſhall paſs over the expence of at leaſt four thouſand bankruptcies, and ten times that number of lawſuits. The different ſums above ſpecified extend to ninety millions ſterling. Let us next put the caſe that this money had been placed at a compound intereſt of five *per cent.* ‖ At the end of ninety-eight years from

---

\* Memoirs of Great Britain and Ireland, part iii. book 10.
† Ibid. part iii. book 5.
‡ Ibid. Part iv. book 1.
§ Macpherſon, vol. ii. chap. 7.
‖ The legal intereſt of money was not reduced from ſix *per cent.* to five, till the twelfth year of Queen Anne. The writer of the Memoirs of Great Britain obſerves, that in thoſe days, parliament found more difficulty in borrowing at *eight* per cent. than we do now in getting money at *four*. Lord North paid, and we have ſtill the ſatisfaction of paying *ſix* or *ſeven* per cent. for the money that ſupported his American war ; and this is known to all mankind, with it ſeems a ſingle exception. At *four* per cent. we could not raiſe a ſingle ſhilling.

the

the peace of Ryfwick, that is to fay in 1795, thefe ninety millions would have doubled themfelves exactly feven times, and the final produce would have been ELEVEN THOUSAND FIVE HUNDRED AND TWENTY MILLIONS STERLING, or a dividend of *eleven hundred and fifty-two pounds* to every individual inhabitant of Britain. This fum is equal to the difcharge of our national debts forty-eight times over, and is five hundred and feventy-five times greater than the whole gold and filver coin at prefent in the three kingdoms. Such has been the price of *a Dutch frontier*, and of *Hudfon's Bay*. As Britain and Ireland are faid to contain an hundred and four thoufand fquare miles, if the money had been employed in the improvements of agriculture, it would have fupplied a fund of *an hundred and one thoufand one hundred and fifty-three pounds fifteen fhillings and eleven pence, and feven thirteenth parts of a penny* for each fquare mile. This fum is much more than upon an average the whole landed property of both iflands is worth *.

An objection may be advanced to this ftatement, that a great part of the fixty millions thus expended by government was *embezzled among ourfelves,* and that as it never actually went out of the country, *we are not at this day a farthing poorer than if the money had never been raifed.* If we might oppofe the language of common fenfe to the jargon of political fophiftry, I would anfwer, that when a grazier in Yorkfhire has been knocked down and robbed, he cares but little whether his guineas are to be ftaked at the gaming tables of Paris or of London. But we fhall admit that the Dutch adminiftration like all thofe which have come after it, was a fcene of inexpreffible infamy; that *thirty millions* out of the *fixty* were pilfered in their road to the fervice of the public; and that the peers and others who ftole this money applied their plunder to ends as honeft as could have been devifed by the farmers and tradefmen who were ftripped of it. This is not very feafible, for what is won in a bad way is com-

* In the Memoirs of Great Britian and Ireland, the author eftimates the mere *lofs of labour* to the contending nations during the nine years of war, at ninety millions Sterling, exclufive of the additional lofs of labour *for life,* by the mutual flaughter.

monly

monly spent in a worse one; but let us proceed. In estimating the expences of the war, there was *omitted* an article of loss at least equivalent to these thirty millions. It has been observed, that a workman can, upon an average, earn about ten shillings a-week, which in London is at present about half the common wages of a journeyman taylor. Reduce this to twenty-five pounds *per annum*, and his life may be estimated at twelve years purchase, or three hundred pounds in value to the public. In the war in question, we lost an hundred thousand men, and by this moderate and simple computation, the price of their blood to Brit..in was not worth less than thirty millions Sterling. Even this number of an hundred thousand lives is most likely far less than the actual destruction. Four thousand merchant ships were taken by the French privateers, and these alone must have required, one with another, twelve or thirteen mariners, which gives us an amount of fifty thousand prisoners; of whom, besides the numbers killed, at least ten or fifteen thousand would perish of jail distempers, of their wounds, of cold or hunger, and above all, of a broken heart.

As the pillage of public money is one of the worst consequences of war, I shall here say something farther on that subject. In 1695, Knight and Duncombe, two members of the House of Commons, were expelled for having forged indorsements on Exchequer bills. Duncombe confessed the charge, and his share of the booty had extended to *four hundred thousand pounds*. I am not informed what was the amount of Knight's plunder; or that of several others who were concerned. The Commons, in a fit of purity, passed a bill to fine Duncombe in half his estate. By the statute laws of England, he should have suffered death. The bill for his fine was rejected in the house of Lords *, by the casting vote of the Duke of Leeds, who was himself a swindler of the first distinction. The Earl of Chesterfield had some reason for terming that house an hospital of *Incurables*. Salmon tells us, that the ministry gave whatever interest and premiums were demanded for the loan of

---

* Memoirs of Great Britain and Ireland, part iii, book 4,

money

money, and that provisions and naval stores were taken up at an advance of thirty, forty, and sometimes fifty *per cent.* above their proper price. But, indeed, after the dimiffion of Mr. Duncombe, *with his four hundred thousand pounds in his pocket,* every charge of this kind becomes perfectly credible.

Whether in the present age, matters have been much mended, there was nobody better able to inform us than the late Earl of Chatham. " There is a set of men," says he, " in the city of " London, who are known to live in riot and luxury, upon the " plunder of the ignorant, the innocent, and the helpless, upon " that part of the community, which ſtands moſt in need of, " and beſt deſerves the care and protection of the legiſlature. " To me, my Lords, whether they be miſerable jobbers of " Change Alley, or the lofty Aſiatic plunderers of Leadenhall " Street, they are all equally deteſtable. I care but little " whether a man walks on foot, or is drawn by eight horſes, " or by ſix horſes ; if his luxury be ſupported by the plunder " of his country, I deſpiſe and abhor him. My Lords, while " I had the honour of ſerving his Majeſty, *I never ventured to* " *look at* THE TREASURY, *but from a diſtance ;* it is a buſineſs " I am unfit for, and to which I never could have ſubmitted. " The little I know of it, has not ſerved to raiſe my opinion " of what is vulgarly called the *monied intereſt ;* I mean that " BLOODSUCKER, that MUCKWORM, which calls itſelf the " friend of Government, which pretends to ſerve this or that " adminiſtration, and may be purchaſed on the ſame terms *by* " *any adminiſtration.* Under this deſcription I include the " whole race of commiſſioners, jobbers, contractors, clothiers, " and remitters *."

The war of 1689 is at this day almoſt forgotten, in the blaze of more recent and ſtupendous follies. Yet the preſent ſhort ſketch of thoſe calamities which it produced, cannot fail of

---

* *Vide* his ſpeech in the debate on Falkland's Iſlands, which has been re-printed in the Anecdotes.

This quarrel ended like others, in our diſappointment, and perhaps diſgrace. Beſides much expence and trouble to individuals, the nation ſquandered between three and four millions ſterling. *Quid vis inſane ?*

leading us into some melancholy reflections on the general tendency of the military fystem. War may produce advantage to a race of barbarians, who have nothing to do, and nothing to lofe; but for a commercial nation, it can be no better than an alderman deferting his ledger, to bet in a cock-pit. Of this fyftem there is no part more injurious than that which enjoins the capture of merchant fhips. An honeft mariner has by the labour of half his life earned a thoufand pounds, and embarks his whole property in a veffel freighted from Leith or Dunkirk. He is boarded by an enemy's privateer; his effects are forfeited; and e himfelf is to rot for fix, or twelve, or eighteen months in a French or Englifh jail; while his wife, his children, or perhaps his father—but this part of the picture becomes too fhocking for the contemplation of humanity. Of thefe matters, kings or courtiers almoft never think. At a certain elevation, the human heart feems to contract a *froft* more impenetrable than the fummit of the Alps or the Andes. It would be an aufpicious event for mankind, if all the fhips of war in the world could be reduced to afhes in one day.

We have adopted a fancy, that frequent hoftilities are unavoidable. Yet the Swifs, a nation of foldiers, and placed in the midft of contending tyrants, have hardly been thrice at war in the courfe of three centuries. The reafon is, that their governments are founded on wifdom, benevolence, and integrity; while ours breathe only maxims of a lefs amiable nature [*]. Other inftances from the hiftory of our own ifland may be adduced to the fame purpofe. " For *more than a century* after the " memorable year 1189, there was no national quarrel, nor na-" tional war between the two kingdoms [†]." This circumftance

[*] " The republics of Europe are all, and we may fay always " in peace. Holland and Switzerland are without wars, foreign " or domeftic; monarchial governments, it is true, are never " long at reft; the crown itfelf is a temptation to enterprifing " *ruffians* at *home*; and that degree of pride and infolence, ever " attendant on regal authority, fwells into a rupture with foreign " powers, in inftances where a republican government, by being " formed on more natural principles, would negociate the ,. miftake." *Common Senfe.*

[†] Annals of Scotland, by Lord Hailes, vol. i. p. 133.

becomes the more remarkable, becaufe, at that time our anceftors were fit for almoft nothing elfe but fighting. The fatal
conteft that began in the end of the thirteenth century, fprung
from the ambition of Edward the Firft. The refpective nations lived in a profound peace, and were alike folicitous to
preferve it.

From the year 1403, to the battle of Flodden, in 1513, being a fpace of *an hundred and ten years,* peace was maintained
between the two kingdoms, with very little interruption ;
though fometimes there was a war which hardly lafted above a
fingle campaign. During the long and bloody ftruggle between
the houfes of York and Lancafter, the Scots interfered only
once or twice at moft, and that was at the earneft defire of
the Englifh exiles ; but they formed no ungenerous and impracticable plans of conqueft. Even to Flodden they were
driven by the temerity of their fovereign ; and his fortunate
death put an inftant end to hoftilities. Our anceftors, whom we
confider as barbarians, were unacquainted with the deliberate
fyftematic thirft of blood which marks a modern politician ; and
what quarrels they had, arofe from the folly of their feveral
monarchs. We have not enjoyed ten years of peace together
fince the Revolution. Even when we ceafe to fight in Europe,
a war muft immediately commence in Afia, or Africa, or America, and in the face of all this work, we call ourfelves the hap-
pieft people in the world.

Peace may be confidered as the univerfal parent of human
happinefs. Induftry cannot long thrive without it, and to this
we are indebted for a great part of our comforts, our enjoy-
ments, and our refources. Spain has long been envied for her
gold and filver mines, which, by Dr. Robertfon's account, have
in two centuries and a half, produced above two thoufand millions fterling. But fober induftry is vaftly more valuable than
all the mines in the world. · If we can forbear butchery, we
need not defpair of difcharging every penny of our public debt,
with eafe, in lefs than a century ; or if we fhould not, ftill the
property of the nation would increafe with fuch rapidity, that
the debt itfelf muft be hardly felt. To make this truth evident,

dent, let us attend to what follows. As a counterpart to the bubble of Falkland's Iflands, four millions fterling have lately been expended on a Spanifh convention. Had they been placed out at five *per cent.* of compound intereft, they would in ninety-eight years have produced five hundred and twelve millions fterling, and at prefent one half of this latter fum would be more than fufficient to difcharge all our incumbrances, and make us as free of debts as our grandfathers were when the Prince of Orange landed. It is true, that the job government of Britain cannot, like that of a Swifs canton, place money at intereft, but from calculations of this fort, we may form a conjecture, as to what we aie capable of faving, by confidering what we have fpent. The American war alone added about one hundred and fifty millions to our public debt, and yet we are in reality a richer nation than when that war began *. Our funds, as we call them, have not hitherto recovered the fhock, but that is, in fpite of common prejudice, a happy circumftance. Had THE YOUNG MAN been able to borrow money with equal facility as his father, we fhould certainly have been fcourged into a Spanifh war. Now, though the country has recovered, and though our commerce is greatly fuperior to what it had ever before been, it is evident, that if we had not poffeffed an almoft inexhauftible vital principle of reproduction and accumulation, fo great a havock of property as an hundred and fifty, or even an hundred millions fterling, muft have reduced whole provinces of this ifland to a defart. Such a complete recovery from the lofs of more than an hundred millions in lefs than ten years, prefents us with a regular annual overplus of at leaft fix

---

* On the fubject of national improvement, the reader may confult with advantage Dr. Campbell's Political Survey of Britain ; an Eftimate of the Comparative Strength of Britain, during the prefent and two preceding reigns, by George Chalmers, Efq. and a continuation of this latter work, by the fame elegant and profound writer, publifhed about fix months ago. Our preffes are groaning under controverfial divinity, heraldy, blank verfe, commentaries on Shakefpeare, and every other imaginable fpecies of nonfenfe, while the books here referred to, have not in this country been honoured, as I am informed, with even a fecond edition.

or

at eight millions. But that we may not overshoot the mark, let us rate the clear annual profits of British commerce and agriculture at only five millions. We shall find that this yearly accumulation of stocks with the legal compound interest only, amounts, in twenty-eight years, to three hundred millions. So that by a peace of twenty-eight years, we shall become a more opulent nation, than we would be at this moment were all our debts paid off to the last farthing.

Before we call this prospect extravagant, let us consider what has actually happened. The most sanguine projector, thirty years ago, would not have presumed to believe that four millions sterling were by this time to be employed in extending and adorning a single city in Scotland. Yet this progress of elegance continues to rise upon us like enchantment. Who in the last century would have suspected that by this time our North American colonies were to contain four millions of inhabitants? It must be owned, that besides other evils, Gibraltar, Canada, Nova Scotia, Botany Bay, the East India Company, and the civil list, are a sort of political millstones hanging at the neck of British prosperity. Yet such are our resources, that if we chuse to desist from the war system, our wealth must in the course of fifty years extend beyond all calculation. Mr. Fox, if providence shall continue to bless us with his abilities till that period, will not then have the smallest difficulty in obtaining a pension of forty thousand pounds a year for every descendant of the royal family. Three ungrateful nations will then cease to affirm, that for his conduct in a certain debate *, any other man would have deserved a flogging at

every

---

* *Vide* his speeches in parliament on the settlement of the Duke of York. If the clerk of a counting-house were to lose at the gaming-table a thousand pounds of his master's money, or even of his own, he would be discharged as unworthy of trust. There is a man, who is said to have lost five hundred thousand pounds in that way; and when he had thus reduced himself to bankruptcy, we have seen him preferred to the management of an annual revenue of sixteen millions sterling. It is difficult to conceive a more gigantic instance of stupidity and depravity than such a choice. That a House of Commons should adopt a mi-

.nister

every whipping-poſt in England. At that happy period, we
ſhall ſupport, without winching, an hundred Lords of the Bed-
chamber, and as many Lords of the Neceſſary Houſe. With
theſe crumbs of comfort, I proceed to the war of the Spaniſh
ſucceſſion, a legacy from our Dutch benefactor.

## CHAP. VI.

England has been the prey of jobs ever ſince the Revolution.
PAINE.

CHARLES the Second King of Spain had no children; he
was of declining years, and a feeble conſtitution. There
were three candidates for the inheritance of his dominions, the
Emperor, the Dauphin of France, and the Electoral Prince of
Bavaria. The Emperor claimed right as male repreſentative

niſter of this ſort, is quite *in character*; but that individuals, who
have the happineſs of their country at heart, ſhould applaud ſuch
a ſelection, muſt fill every ſober man with aſtoniſhment. To
ſweep off large ſums at the gaming-table, is a diſhonourable
dirty practice. Mr. Fox, in the boundleſs diverſity of his adventures, muſt have ruined many a family, and ſent many a
helpleſs woman with ſorrow to the grave.
  In the manuſcript of a tour in Switzerland, which I have ſeen,
the following paſſage deſerves peculiar attention. " At Bern,
" a heavy penalty is impoſed upon any perſon, who in one day
" ſhall loſe more than two pounds five ſhillings ſterling by gam-
" ing; and every member of government, and officer in public
" ſervice, is obliged to take an oath, not only that he ſhall faith-
" fully and honourably obſerve this law, but that he ſhall zea-
" louſly maintain it, and that he ſhall freely and impartially give
" information againſt all perſons who to his knowledge ſhall
" offend againſt it. The preſence of ſome of thoſe diſtinguiſh-
" ed perſons in all good companies, proves in fact an invincible
" bar to immoderate play." With what contemptuous pity
would a Swiſs hear us prattling, that our government is the
*envy* of the world !

F                                    to

to the family of Auſtria. Philip the Fourth, predeceſſor and father to Charles, had left behind him two daughters by different marriages. The eldeſt was mother to the Dauphin ; the youngeſt had eſpouſed the Emperor, and their daughter, an only ſurviving child, had been married to the Elector of Bavaria, to whom ſhe had born that Prince who was at preſent a candidate. It ſeems that the Dauphin of France, as deſcending from the eldeſt daughter of Phillip the Fourth, had the neareſt right ; but as the other nations of Europe were extremly jealous of France, it was early foreſeen that the Dauphin's claim would meet with a dangerous oppoſition. On the 1ſt of October 1698, the King of France, the King of England, and the Republic of Holland, engaged in a contract as to this ſucceſſion. Their bargain was, that the Dauphin ſhould ſucceed to the kingdoms of Naples and Sicilly, and a certain portion of the provinces of Spain itſelf. The other two candidates were to ſhare the reſt of the dominions, and this agreement hath ſince been called the *firſt* treaty of partition. So vaſt an acceſſion of territory would have rendered France a moſt formidable neighbour to the Dutch, and on their part the treaty ſeems to have be· n act of imprudence. The ſecret of this combination having come to light, Charles in a rage inſtantly made a teſtament, by which he transferred the whole dominions of Spain, to the young Prince of Bavaria. But as the latter died ſoon after, he made a ſecond will, by which he bequeathed the ſucceſſion, alſo entire, to the Archduke Charles, the Emperor's ſecond ſon, by a marriage which he had entered into after the death of his Spaniſh empreſs. The former parties, on the 14th March 1700, engaged in a *ſecond* treaty of partition, by which the Dauphin was to receive a large addition to his ſhare, and the remainder was reſerved for the Emperor. This tranſaction alſo reached Charles, before it was cloſed ; and in Auguſt 1699, his ambaſſador at London delivered to the Engliſh miniſtry an intereſting appeal on the conduct of William. He remarked, that if ſuch proceedings were allowed, no people, no dominion could be ſafe againſt the ambition of the ſtrongeſt, and the deceits of the moſt malicious ; that ſhould ſtrangers be ſuffered to put their hands into the lines

of

of fucceffion of kings, no ftatutes, no municipal laws would be obferved ; that no crown could be free from the attempts of aliens; and the crown of England lefs than any crown; and that were men to lie watching for the ficknefs of fovereigns, no health could be conftant, and no life fecure. He alfo reminded them, that the expences of a war, and the deftruction of commerce, muft be the certain confequence of fuch adventures.

For this honeft production, the ambaffador was forced to leave England. On the 2d of October 1700, the King of Spain, by the advice of the Pope, made a third teftament. To put an end to all projects of a partition, he left the whole empire, undivided, to the Duke of Anjou, the fecond fon of the Dauphin of France, and grandfon to Lewis the Fourteenth. By this choice, he attempted to avert the calamities of a difputed fucceffion. For as the Duke of Anjou was not heir to the crown of France, that circumftance removed the objection of making a hazardous augmentation to the French dominions. This meafure was more fimble, juft, and practicable, than that adopted by William and the Dutch. On the 25th November 1700, Charles died ; and though he bequeathed fuch a fplendid legacy to the houfe of Bourbon, he had been one of William's allies in his laft long and bloody war againft France ; a fact which evinces the mutability of the political world.

On the death of their fovereign, the Spanifh nation determined that a confpiracy of foreigners fhould not be fuffered to partition their provinces. They difpatched a courier to the court of France with the teftament of their late fovereign, and if Lewis fhould refufe to accept the monarchy for his grandfon, they gave him orders to proceed to Vienna, and make an offer of the univerfal fucceffion to the Archduke. Thus Lewis had his choice of two meafures. If he accepted the teftament of Charles, his grandfon was at once, and without oppofition, put into poffeffion of the Spanifh dominions, at the hazard of a quarrel with the Dutch and England. If he refufed this offer, the Auftrian Archduke was with equal certainty to afcend the throne, and Lewis was to depend on the very doubtful friendfhip of his old enemies, the Dutch and England, for their affift-

ance

ance to conquer a fhare of Spain, in oppofition to the Emperor and that nation. But as Lewis himfelf was feared and hated both i Hollana and England, there is not the leaft probability, t at he would have obtained any ferious aid in his pretenfions, from the two countries. We cannot therefore with reafon condemn him, when he accepted for the Duke of Anjou the offer of the Spanifh crown. The reader is requefted to pay par-ticular attention to this concife and candid ftate of the cafe; for even at prefent, it is the vulgar opinion that Lewis acted upon this occafion with treachery. It would be more proper to fay, that William engaged in an enterprife far above his power, and that he fhewed an utter indifference to the intereft of his kingdoms. The preference which the Spanifh nation be-ftowed upon the Duke of Anjou, was in the moral fenfe an am-ple vindication of the acceptance of Lewis. If there be fuch a thing as equity upon earth, it muft begin with this maxim, that a people are at all times entitled to their choice of a mafter.

On the 17th of April 1701, William acknowledged the Duke of Anjou, as the lawful fovereign of Spain, by a letter under his own hand. The Dutch alfo recognized his right. On the 7th of September thereafter, William, with his wonted confift-ency, entered into an alliance with the Emperor and Holland to attack the young monarch. The defign avowed in the ar-ticles was, to obtain the Dutchy of Milan from the crown of Spain, as a compenfation to the Emperor; and Flanders, or part of it, as a barrier for Holland. What England was to ob-tain, we are not informed. On the 6th of September 1701, James the Second expired, and Lewis, on his death, acknow-ledged his fon as King of England. Though this was but an empty form, William employed it as a pretence to feduce the nation into a fecond war. His project was embraced with exul-tation by all parties.

Yet though Lewis was to blame, we ourfelves had behaved but little better. Our affumed title as *King of France*, is not only a difhonourable untruth, but a wanton infult to a refpectable people. William prepared for a campaign, but happily both for others and himself, a fall from his horse put an end to his battles and his treaties, on the 8th of March 1702 *.

Before we enter into the events of this war, it may not be improper to illuftrate, by an exact and interefting parallel, what Dr. Swift calls " our *infamous* treaty of partition." Let us fuppofe, that for fome years before the death of Queen Elizabeth, all Europe had forefeen that fhe was to die childlefs, that James the Sixth of Scotland was to be her fucceffor, and that by fuch an increafe of dominion, England was to enfure a decifive addition of power and importance. " No," exclaimed the Dutch, the French, and the Auftrians, " we cannot, Elizabeth, " permit you and your people to chufe a fovereign for Eng- " land. We all know that *Mafter* † James is a fool. He has " married a daughter of the King of Denmark ; and hence " the Britifh Empire would become but a province to the " court of Copenhagen, We have formed a much better plan, " and you muft adopt it. Jerfey, Guernfey, and Plymouth, " Dover caftle, and the county of Kent, are to compofe a " frontier in the hands of his Moft Chriftian Majefty. The

---

* In drawing up this ftatement, Mr. Macpherfon has been chiefly followed, with fome additions from the Memoirs of Great Britain and Ireland, printed in 1788. In this laft work, William is every where reprefented as a virtuous and fublime character. The ftory of the Countefs of Orkney, and the trite cataftrophe of Darien, with many others of the fame fort, are completely explained away. The partition treaties are defended, as pregnant with future bleffings to England ; for the hiftorian feems to fancy that the Allies could have divided the provinces of Spain, with the exactnefs and tranquillity of a grocer cutting a pound of cheefe. The fequel fufficiently proved the abfurdity of fuch a fuppofition,

This writer has affigned a remarkable reafon for fending into the world his fecond volume. " But feeing England lately, as " I thought, on the brink of ruin, becaufe fhe was on the brink " of a *continental war*, I thought that the pictures of mifery, " even amid fuccefs, which the continental wars of the two " grand alliances prefent, might make the public attend to *the* " *profpect before them.*"

It is impoffible to publifh from more honourable motives, or to atteft a more important truth.

† Henry the Fourth of France ufed to call him fo.

" ifles of Wight, Anglefea, and Man, muft be delivered up to
" their High Mightineffes for the convenience of importing
" gin ; and you muft likewife permit them to catch and cure
" pilchards on the ceaft of Cornwall. To Ireland you never
" had any title but that of a robber, and as you are deteſted
" by the whole nation, to the very laſt man, it is neceſſary, for
" preferving *the balance of power*, to declare them independent.
" As for the reſt of your dominions, we have brought you a
" GERMAN maſter, born at the diſtance of a thouſand miles,
" a ſtranger to your country, your laws, your manners, and
" your language. In defence of *his* RIGHT, we have difem-
" barked on the coaſt of Yorkſhire two hundred thouſand
" armed ruffians ; and unleſs you inſtantly acknowledge him
" as ſucceſſor, we ſhall ſpread defolation from Caithneſs to the
" land's end. If his Daniſh majeſty declines to affift us in
" overwhelming his fon-in-law, our admirals have orders to
" beat Copenhagen about his ears. We are perfectly deter-
" mined ; and before we give up the point, we ſhall ſpend the
" laſt drop of our blood, and the laſt farthing of our money ;
" befides diving into more debt than our poſterity can pay off
" in an hundred generations."

On the 4th of May 1702, hoſtilities were declared againſt
Spain. " We haſtily engaged in a war," ſays Swift, " which
" hath coſt us SIXTY MILLIONS, and after repeated, as well as
" *unexpected* ſucceſs in arms, hath put us and our poſterity in a
" worſe condition, not only than any of our allies, but than
" even *our conquered enemies themſelves* \*." The two firſt campaigns escaped without any decifive event. On the 25th of
November 1702, the Commons, in confequence of a mendicant
meffage from the Court, affigned the yearly ſum of an hundred
thouſand pounds to the Prince of Denmark, her Majeſty's

---

\* The Conduct of the Allies. This is the cafe at the end of
almoſt every war, and reminds me of a remark made by Lord
Monboddo. Somebody once aſked him, Whether Europe or
America had profited moſt by the difcoveries of Columbus ?
" The balance," replied his Lordſhip, " is pretty equal. We
" gave them *brandy* and *the ſmall-pox*; and they gave us *rum*
" and *the great pox*."

hufband,

hufband, in cafe he fhould furvive her. So extravagant a penfion confirms the remark of Milton, that *the trappings of a monarchy would fet up an ordinary commonwealth.* On the 28th of October 1708, the Prince died, and as he was a perfon of the moft innocent character, it founds harfhly to fay, that his exit was defirable. Yet had he outlived Anne, twenty thoufand neceffitous families muft each have paid five pounds a year of their pittance to fupport him. And this fingle impofition would, while it lafted, have comprehended more fubftantial injuftice and oppreffion than all the other thefts and robberies in the country.

In September 1703, Charles, the fecond fon of the Emperor Leopold, was declared King of Spain, and as fuch, was acknowledged by all the Allies, including the Dutch and England, who had both formerly recognized the title of the French Prince. It is needlefs to expatiate on the juftice or decency of fuch a meafure. In Auguft 1704, Marlborough won the battle of Blenheim. In October 1706 Lewis offered better terms of pacification *than were afterwards excepted.* With what propriety then are we to blame *his* ambition ? " The Whigs," fays Mr. Macpherfon, " who were now poffeffed of the whole " power of government in England, *infulted common fenfe,* in the " reafon which they gave for rejecting the propofed peace. " They faid, that the terms offered by France were TOO GOOD, " to be the foundation for a lafting tranquillity, and therefore " they ought not be admitted."—Had Lewis engaged to reftore Normandy to England, that, upon *Whig* principles, would have been a ftill better reafon for refufing an agreement. Such were the political heroes whofe *virtues* we vaunt of adopting, and by whom Europe was condemned to remain for fix years and five months longer, a fcene of confufion, diftrefs, and carnage ! This infolence very foon met with its reward. On the 25th of April 1707, an entire *Whig* army was difperfed, taken, or extirpated, at Almanza, by the Duke of Berwick. Sixteen thoufand of the vanquifhed were killed or made prifoners. In this campaign, the Duke of Marlborough atchieved nothing worthy of his former fame. Prince Eugene, with forty
thoufand

thousand men, invaded Provence, and invested Toulon. His forces were in danger of being surrounded, and his escape or flight was marked with the usual and heroic circumstances of slaughter and devastation. Four English men of war, with Admiral Shovel, a person whose abilities had raised him from the rank of a common sailor, foundered on the rocks of Scilly. In short, the disasters of the Allies were so numerous and severe, that Lewis might at this time have turned the chase, if his counsels had not been governed by an old woman. The Scots, by a bargain sufficiently questionable had been *united* with England. The whole nation were inflamed into a degree of madness. The Pretender's birth day was publicly celebrated at Edinburgh ; and a memorial was transmitted to France by a number of nobility and gentry, who promised to embody in his favour five thousand horse and twenty-five thousand foot. The proposal was rejected. In 1708, the Allies were more successful, and among other blessed events, they gained Lisle, with the loss of eighteen or twenty thousand men. For what notable purposes have we dragged the smith from his anvil, and the farmer from his plow ! In 1709, the Government borrowed from the Bank of England four hundred thousand pounds, at six *per cent.* besides granting them several advantages, which may have raised the real interest to ten or twelve *per cent.* and all this for the pleasure of making a German King of Spain. The practice of advancing money to the public was at that time, and has been ever since, a very profitable traffick to those gentlemen of whom Lord Chatham has made such honourable mention. Lewis, in the beginning of this year, had renewed his offers of peace. He attempted, as Torcy relates, to bribe the Duke of Marlborough, by a conditional present of four millions of livres ; but his Grace, after due consideration, declined the proposal. The aged and unfortunate King promised *to yield the whole Spanish monarchy to the House of Austria without any equivalent* *. He consented to a series of the most degrading demands which his enemies could

---

* Macpherson, vol. ii. chap. 7.

Invent, but they left him no choice between refiftance and deftruction. France was in the mean time ravaged by a terrible famine, which ferved to fill up the meafure of univerfal wretch-
ednefs. Whatever we may think of Lewis himfelf, and even a
defpot may deferve our pity, one muft have the nerves of a
Dutchman or a *Whig*, if he does not feel for the miferies of
twenty millions of people. On the 10th of September 1709,
thefe conferences were fucceeded by the victory of Malplaquet,
which Marlborough purchafed with the lives of twenty thoufand
men, while the French, though *defeated*, left but eigh thoufand
dead on the field.

In 1710, Lewis made frefh offers of fubmiffion. " He pro-
" mifed even a fubfidy of a million of livres monthly to the
" Allies, till King Philip *fhould be driven out of Spain*\*." But
mark what follows :—They required that Lewis fhould affift
them *with all his forces*, to expel his grandfon from the throne
of that kingdom. We need not enlarge upon the bafenefs of
trampling a fallen adverfary, fince our illuftrious anceftors might
have improved their morality from a boxing ftage. A ring of
chairmen would be afhamed of fuch confummate barbarity.
Whether Lewis would have fubmitted to this laft act of degra-
dation is doubtful, for Eugene and Marlborough obftructed the
progrefs of explanation, and commenced the campaign.—
" They gained three places of importance, and conquered
" twelve leagues of a fine country. But they loft twenty-fix
" thoufand men by the fword. *Half their infantry was ruined*
" *by wounds, difeafes, and fatigue* †." In Spain, we obtained
during this year two victories. Stanhope, the Englifh general,
entered Madrid. " The army lived at large upon the people,
" without order, without moderation, and without difcipline.
" They raifed contributions on private perfons. *They pillaged*
" *the churches, and fold publicly the utenfils of the altar* ‡."
Nobody can be forry to hear that on the 8th of December 1710,
thefe ruffians were defeated. Stanhope himfelf was taken prifoner, with five thoufand Britifh troops.

---

\* Macpherfon, vol. ii. chap. 7.  † Ibid.  ‡ Ibid.

G  By

By this time the nation were almost tired with the expence of this war, and had begun to suspect the absurdity of its first principles. But as the Cabinet was comletely garrisoned by the partisans of Marlborough, to reverse the system, required both a strong and dexterous hand. A circumstance in itself trifling contributed to this event; and the friends of mankind must acknowledge, that for once at least, public happiness has been promoted by public superstition. On the 3d of November 1709, Henry Sacheverell, a Tory parson, preached at St. Paul's a sermon, in which he enforced, with much virulence, the nonsense about passive obedience and non-resistance. In this performance, the Earl of Godolphin, Lord High Treasurer of England, and one of the chief leaders of the Whigs, was personally attacked, and the whole party were eager to punish the man who had thus contested their darling doctrines. They brought him to a trial before the House of Peers; and this measure gave the Tories an opportunity for asserting *that the Church was in danger.* The great body of the people broke into a transport of rage. " The current, which had been long chang- " ing, ran down with a force, that levelled every thing before it*." During the trial, the pews of five dissenting meeting-houses were burnt in the streets. The outrages of the rabble were directed by persons of higher rank, who attended at their heels in hackney coaches; the watch word was—*The Church and Sacheverell.* Those who joined not in the shout were insulted and knocked down; and Burnet tells us, that at his door one man got his skull cleft with a spade, for his refusal. The sermon was ordered to be burnt by the hangman, but the public flame was kept up with much address by the Tories. Sacheverell made a journey into Wales, and was every where received with raptures of admiration. The Queen, by degrees, embraced this opportunity to free herself from the tyranny of an insolent faction. On the 8th of August 1710, Godolphin was dismissed. A new parliament was summoned to meet on the 25th of November thereafter. The frenzy of the

* Macpherson, vol. ii. chap. 8.

mob was fupported by the fubftantial logic of the Treafury; and a majority was returned of Tory members. Harley, the new minifter, and his affociates, had too much fenfe to difcover abruptly their defigns to the people. The fum of fourteen millions five hundred and feventy-three thoufand, three hundred and nineteen pounds, nineteen fhillings and eight pence halfpenny, was voted to difcharge the arrears in the navy and other offices, and the fervices of the current year. At this critical moment, a fecond ftroke of fortune advanced the pacific views of the Tories. On the 1ft of May 1705, the Emperor Leopold had died; and on the 6th of April 1711, his eldeft fon and fucceffor, Jofeph, died alfo; and without regarding his own two daughters, left his brother Charles, *our intended King of Spain*, his univerfal heir. " His death *fuddenly changed the whole* " *ftate of affairs.* The war undertaken by the grand alliance " for preferving the balance of Europe, was now *likely to de-* " *ftroy it for ever;* and men who judged of the future by the " paft, began to dread the irrefiftible power of the Emperor " Charles the Fifth, in the perfon of a prince of his family *." Hence, *even upon our own mad principles*, it became juft as neceffary to oppofe the fucceffion of our candidate Charles, as that of the Duke of Anjou. Yet with the moft aftonifhing impudence, the Whigs and our Allies, Charles and the Dutch, were anxious to continue the war. The German princes, and among others, the Elector of Hanover †, expreffed their higheft difapprobation of the projected peace. The arguments of George, if fuch they may be called, are too frivolous for confutation or infertion here. Portugal and Savoy feconded the German chorus. " The emoluments derived from war were greater " than their expectations from peace.—The money of the ma- " ritime powers, and chiefly that of England, more than the " territories of the Houfe of Bourbon, was the grand object of " thofe petty tyrants, who *fed on the blood of fubjects whom they*

---

* Macpherfon, vol. i. chap. 8.
† In a Memorial printed by his envoy, and a letter from himfelf to Harley, dated November 7, 1711.

" let

" *let out for slaughter* \*." Compared with merchants of this de-
scription, an ordinary offender is a paragon of innocence. When
a nation sends for sovereigns from such a school, there appears
but a melancholy presage of the prospect before it.

The campaign of 1711, elapsed without effort on either
side. The surrender of Bouchain on the :3th of September,
closed the military exploits of the Duke of Marlborough. The
new minister of England had been engaged in attempting to re-
concile the demands of the contending powers. But the States
of Holland were so much exasperated by the conduct of Queen
Anne, that they were at no pains in concealing their design to
treat her as they had treated her father. They proposed " to
" fit out a fleet to assist the Elector of Hanover to strike the
" sceptre from her hand †." On the 7th of December, parliament met. Harley had secured a Tory majority in the House
of Commons; but his party was somewhat inferior in the House
of Peers. Affairs had now come to a crisis. The leaders of
the Whigs were suspected of intending an immediate appeal to
arms. It became therefore necessary to dismiss the Duke of
Marlborough from his military command; and on the last day
of December, Harley produced what is now called *a batch of*
*peers.* Twelve gentlemen devoted to the court were created
members of the Upper House. Anne had the very same right
to have created twelve thousand. The constitution of Britain,
like the sword of Dionysius, hangs by a single hair.

On the 17th of January 1712, Mr. Walpole was committed
to the Tower. He had received five hundred guineas, and a
note for five hundred more, for two contracts when secretary at
war, for supplying the forces in Scotland with forage. " A
" member," says Burnet, " who was a Whig, was expelled
" the House; and a prosecution was ordered against him :—but
" *the abuse goes on still, as avowedly as ever*." The Duke of
Marlborough's conduct underwent a severe censure, and Car-

---

\* Macpherson, vol. ii. chap. 8. Seventeen thousand of these
miserable victims were at one time furnished by the Court of
Hanover. *Macpherson's State Papers*, vol. ii. p. 497.
† Macpherson, vol. ii. chap. 8.

donnel,

donnel, his fecretary, was expelled by the Commons. The
campaign of 1712 was unfortunate on the part of the Allies.
The Britifh forces under the command of the Duke of Ormond
remained inactive ; and even the abfence of the abilities of Marlborough feems to have been feverely felt, The peace was not
finally fettled till March 1713. The Whig faction, to their
eternal infamy, ftrained every nerve to prevent it, By this
peace, befides the iflands of Minorca and St. Chriftopher's, and
the fortrefs of Gibraltar, for ourfelves, we obtained the ifland
of Sicily for the Duke of Savoy, which produced the Spanifh
war in 1718, a partial right for our merchants of trading to
South America, which began the Spanifh war of 1739, and
Nova Scotia, which gave rife to the French war in 1756.
This war was more deftructive than that of 1689, as it
lafted for eleven campaigns. Dr. Swift computes that each
of them coft us fix or feven millions fterling. The lofs of
lives and of fhipping could be hardly, if at all inferior to
that of the former war, as our battles were numerous, and
as the protection of our commerce was altogether neglected.
In a word, the nation fquandered feventy or eighty millions,
that Marlborough might pilfer *one*.

To Dr. Swift we are much indebted for the termination of
this war. His pamphlet on *The Conduct of the Allies*, excited
a fort of political earthquake, and more th   all his admirable
verfes muft endear him to diftant pofterity. A few paffages
may ferve as a fpecimen of the reft, " It will appe.," fays
he, " by plain matters of fact, that no nation was ever fo long,
" or fo fcandaloufly abufed, by the folly, the temerity, the
" corruption, and the ambition of its domeftic enemies ; or
" treated with fo much infolence, injuftice, and ingratitude, by
" its foreign friends.—We are deftroying many thoufand lives,
" and exhaufting our fubftance, not for our own intereft, which
" would be but common prudence ; not for a thing indifferent,
" which would be fufficient folly ; but perhaps to our own de-
" ftruction, which is perfect madnefs,—The common queftion
" is, if we muft now furrender Spain, what have we been fight-
" ing for all this while ? The anfwer is ready. We have been
" fighting for the ruin of the public intereft, and the advance-
" ment

" ment of a private. We have been fighting to raise the
" wealth and grandeur of a particular family ;" (that of Marlborough,) " to enrich usurers and stockjobbers, and to culti-
" vate the pernicious designs of a faction, by destroying the
" landed interest.—Since the monied men are so fond of war,
" I should be glad if they would furnish out one campaign *at*
" *their own charge.* It is not above six or seven millions ; and
" I dare engage to make it out, that, *when they have done this,*
" instead of contributing equal to the landed men, they will
" have their full principal and interest at six *per cent.* remaining
" of all the money they ever lent to the government."

Even at this day, we are deafened about the glorious victories
of the Duke of Marlborough, and though by the death of the
Emperor Joseph, the object of dispute was utterly extinguished,
a crowd of authors persist in lamenting that our commander
was checked in the career of pillage and butchery. Happy
might it have been for this country, had Marlborough, with
all his forces, perished on the field of Blenheim ; since it may
be supposed, that such a stroke would at once have blasted our
crusades upon the continent. As if his Grace had not enjoyed
sufficient opportunities of plundering the treasury of the nation,
as if the manor of Woodstock, the palace of Blenheim *, and an
hundred thousand pounds a year †, had not been adequate to
the services of himself and his Duchess, we are saddled with
an annual payment of five thousand pounds to his family for
ever. When a constitution, deserving that name, shall succeed
our present political anarchy, it is not difficult to foresee some
of the first objects of reformation. The Earl of Chatham enjoys four thousand pounds a year, because his father added se-
venty millions to the national debt. The Duke of Richmond
raises from the city of London an annual revenue, said to be

---

* Dr. Swift estimates Woodstock at forty thousand pounds,
and adds, that Blenheim House had cost two hundred thousand
pounds, and was at the time of his writing *unfinished.* There
can be no wonder, that we must now pay nine-pence per pound
of importation duty for Peruvian bark, and three guineas for
leave to shoot a partridge worth two-pence.

† The sum has been stated higher, but such computations are
always in part random.

twenty thoufand pounds, becaufe he is defcended from the fon of a criminal *, who deferved an hundred t nes over to have been flogged out of human fociety.

As a commentary on the preceding narrative, we may confult a quotation from Dr. Johnfon's pamphlet on Falkland's iflands. The reflections which it contains have more than once extorted, in my hearing, the admiration of the late Dr. Adam Smith, who was far from being a general advocate for this Author.

" It is wonderful, with what coolnefs and indifference the " greater part of mankind fee war commenced. Thofe who " hear of it at a diftance, or read of it in books, but have never " prefented its evils to their minds, confider it as little more " than a fplendid game, a proclamation, an army, a battle, and " a triumph. Some indeed muft perifh in the moft fuccefsful " field, but they die upon the bed of honour, *refign their lives* " *amidft the joys of conqueft, and, filled with England's glory, fmile* " *in death.*

" The life of a modern foldier is ill reprefented by heroic " fiction. War has means of deftruction more formidable than " the cannon and the fword. Of the thoufands and ten thou- " fands who perifhed in our late contefts with France and Spain, " a very fmall part ever felt the ftroke of an enemy ; the reft " languifhed in tents and fhips, amidft damps and putrefaction ; " pale, torpid, fpiritlefs, and helplefs ; gafping and groaning, " unpitied among men, made obdurate by a long continuance " of hopelefs mifery ; and were at laft whelmed in pits, or " heaved into the ocean, without notice, and without remem- " brance. By incommodious encampments, and unwholefome " ftations, where courage is ufelefs, and enterprife impractica- " ble, fleets are filently difpeopled †, and armies fluggifhly " melted away.

" Thus

* Charles II.

† The manning of a fleet has often produced almoft as much mifchief as its *depopulation*. On this fubject there is here fubjoin-ed a fhort but fhocking ftory, which happened about the time when

" Thus is a people gradually exhausted, for the most part
" with little effect. The wars of civilized nations make very
slow

---

when Dr. Johnson's pamphlet was first printed, and which can
hardly be regarded as a digression, since it reflects additional horror on the war system.

A workman, in London, was apprehended by a press gang.
His wife and child were turned to the door by their landlord.
Within a few days after she was delivered of a second child in
a garret. On her recovery, she was driven to the streets
as a common beggar. She went into a shop, and attempted to
carry off a small piece of linen. She was seized, tried, and
condemned to be hanged. In her defence she said, that she
had lived creditably and happy, till a press gang robbed her of
her husband, and in him, of all means to support herself and her
family; and that in attempting to clothe her new born infant,
she perhaps did wrong, as she did not, at that time, know what
she did. The parish officers, and other witnesses, bore testi-
mony to the truth of her averment, but all to no purpose. She
was ordered for Tyburn. *The hangman dragged her sucking infant from her breast, when he strained the cord about her neck.*
On the 13th May 1777, Sir William Meredith mentioned this
assassination in the House of Commons. " Never," said he,
" was there a fouler murder committed against the law, than that
" of this woman by the law."—Such were the fruits of what
Englishmen call *their inestimable privilege of a trial by jury.*
It would not be difficult to fill a large volume with decisions
of this stamp, though there is not perhaps any single case, which
is in all its circumstances so absolutely infernal. The reader
may compare the *guilt,* as it was termed, of Mary Jones, with
the progress of those *noble patriots,* whose history is recorded in
the next chapter, and who are at this day held up as the sa-
viours of Britain, and then say which of the two parties best deserved a halter.

General Gunning, a man who is not worth a shilling, was
lately fined in five thousand pounds for seducing a doxy who
was as forward as himself; and Mr. Tattersal, the editor of
a London newspaper has just now been fined in four thousand
pounds for a paragraph which asserted, that a lady had an
amour with her footman. It was proved that Mr. Tattersal
was at a great distance from London, when this story was printed; and consequently, that had it been even a forgery on the
Bank of England, the law could not have touched a hair of his
head. There can be no doubt that the lady will accept the last
farthing assigned by this verdict, and such an acceptance can
leave no striking impression of female generosity. Another
splendid

"flow changes in the fyſtem of empire. The public perceives
"fcarcely any alteration but an increaſe of debt; and the few
"individuals who are benefited, are not fuppoſed to have the
"cleareſt right to their advantages. If he who ſhared the
"danger enjoyed the profit, and after bleeding in the battle
"grew rich by the victory, he might ſhew his gains without,
"envy. But at the concluſion of a ten year's war, how are we
"recompenſed for the death of multitudes, and the expence of
"millions, but by contemplating the ſudden glories of pay-
"maſters and agents, contractors and commiſſaries, whoſe equi-
"pages ſhine like meteors, and whoſe palaces riſe like exhala-
"tions.

"The are the men who, without virtue, labour, or hazard,
"are growing rich as their country is impoveriſhed; they re-
"joice when obſtinacy or ambition adds another year to
"ſlaughter and devaſtation; and laugh from their deſks at
"bravery and ſcience, while they are adding figure to figure,
"and cipher to cipher, hoping for a new contract from a new
"armament, and computing the profits of a fiege or a tem-
"peſt."

---

ſplendid ſpecimen of an Engliſh jury ſhall conclude this long
note.

Some years ago, Mr. Cooper, of London, was accuſed of
being the printer and publiſher of a performance deemed a
libel. Upon ſtrict inquiry, it was found, that it had been
printed at his office; but it was proved, that at the time when
this was done, he was in ſo dangerous a ſtate of health, as to be
given up by the phyſician who attended him, and that for ſeveral months before the publication, as well as at that period, he
had been entirely diſabled by ſickneſs from either attending his
office, or knowing what was doing in it. Notwithſtanding
theſe circumſtances, a Middleſex jury found him guilty; and, as
foon as he had recovered from his ſickneſs, he was placed on the
pillory, and, no doubt, would have been pelted by miniſterial
hirlings, had not a number of reſpectable gentlemen prevented
it by their perſonal attendance.—So much for the liberty of the
preſs, when protected by a Middleſex jury.

CHAP.

## CHAP. VII.

Where I have treated high life with freedom, I hope I shall not
be underſtood to propagate the doctrine of levellers.—I have
no ſuch intention.—I mean to give a juſt picture of human
life, according to my own knowledge of it, and according to
my ſenſe of truth, without ceremony or diſguiſe.—I do not
wiſh, in any degree, to diminiſh the reſpect which is juſtly
due to perſons and families of diſtinction.

*Letter to the People of Laurencekirk.*

THERE is not in hiſtory a more ſignal example of ingratitude, than the conduct of the Emperor, the Dutch, and
Marlborough, to the Queen of England. She had fought for
ten years the battles of her Allies. She had advanced her general to be the firſt ſubject in Europe. When ſhe refuſed to
complete the ruin of her country for the caprice of the former,
when the inſolence of the latter compelled her to diſmiſs him,
loaded with the plunder of nations, from her preſence, theſe
worthy aſſociates conſpired for the deſtruction of their bene-
factreſs. It is not certain that William himſelf had ever pro-
ceeded into ſuch a climax of baſeneſs. Though his partition
treaties were abſurd in a Britiſh ſovereign, we may forgive, in
his hoſtilities with Lewis, the reſentment of a Dutchman. When
we peruſe the plan of Eugene for ſetting fire to the ſtreets of
London, and the palace of St. James's *, even his tranſcendant
behaviour at the Revolution almoſt fades before it.

By the prudence and firmneſs of Harley, the plots of Eugene
were diſcovered and diſappointed ; and on the 17th of March
1712, he was obliged to embark with ſome precipitation for
the Continent. The neutrality of the Engliſh forces in the
next campaign, with the final termination of the war, has already been mentioned. It does not appear that the Elector of
Hanover was engaged in the ſcheme of dethroning Anne. His

---

* Macpherſon, vol. 2, chap. 9.

beggarly

beggarly condition may have contributed to the moderation of his sentiments. In 1713, he solicited from the English Crown a pension for his mother the Princess Sophia. " In the present " situation of his affairs, a fresh supply of revenue was much " wanted. His agents every where complained of their too " scanty allowance. The Whigs, with all their patriotism, " *were soliciting for pensions.* Some *Lords,* who were zealous " for the Protestant succession, were, it seems, *poor to follow* " *their consciences. They had sold their votes to the Ministry.* " But—*they would take smaller sums from* HIS ELECTORAL " HIGHNESS. The Earl of Sunderland, in his attachment to " the family of Brunswick, had advanced three hundred pounds " to one of these poor *conscientious* Lords. The Earl wished *to* " *see this sum repaid.* Though the Elector might be willing to " gratify such faithful friends, he had reason to expect that " *they would help to serve themselves.* They were, therefore " desired to promote, with all their influence, the pension de- " manded for the Princess. His Highness was no stranger, " upon the present occasion, either to the abilities or poverty of " the Duke of Argyle. The whole world knew his love of " money. He desired that nobleman, and his brother the Earl " of Ilay, to promote the allowance to the Electress, as *they* " *might expect good pensions to themselves from that fund* *.*" This pension was never obtained; and the Electress herself died about sixteen months after, on the 28th of May 1714. " The Elector " himself seems to have become indifferent concerning the suc- " cession of his family to the throne. Teazed by the unmean- " ing professions of the Tories, and harassed by the demands of " the Whigs, he dropped all correspondence with both parties. " He suffered his servants to continue their intrigues in Lon- " don. He listened to their intelligence. But to the requisi- " tions of his Whiggish friends for money, *he turned a deaf* " *ear.* He was however persuaded at length, to order six hun- " dred pounds to the Lord Fitzwalter, to enable that NEEDY

---

* Macpherson, vol. ii. chap. 9. and Hanover Papers, January 27, 1713.

" PEER to pay a debt of three hundred pounds to Sunderland.
" *He allowed forty pounds to the author of a newspaper, for con-*
" *veying to the public, paragraphs favourable to* THE PROTES-
" TANT SUCCESSION. He added ten pounds to that *(immense)*
" *fum, after various representations from his council and fer-*
" *vants* *."—" The excluded party in Britain haraffed, at the
" fame time, the Elector, with propofals *for his invading the*
" *kingdom with a body of troops.* They fuggefted, that fhould
" the Dutch refufe a fquadron of men of war, fome fhips of
" force might be obtained from Denmark. But the Elector
" rejected the fcheme, as utterly improper and impracticable †."

On the 9th of April 1713, the Queen opened a feffion of
parliament. The ftream of popularity had now turned againft
the Whigs. " In this diftrefsful fituation, they implored
" Kreyenbeg to lay their humble folicitations *at the feet* of the
" Elector. They entreated his Highnefs, for the fake of Hea-
" ven, to fend over the Electoral Prince. Without the pre-
" fence of one of the family, they folemnly averred, that the
" fucceffion muft inevitably be defeated ‡." All this canting
had very little foundation in fact. The bulk of the nation
were determined in favour of the Proteftant fucceffion. But
thefe fycophants wifhed to make themfelves of importance with
George the Firft. The following paffage will fet the nature
and motives of their conduct in a proper light.

" The Whigs had, in the beginning of the year (1713) ha-
" raffed the Elector with demands of *penfions* for POOR LORDS.
" They had perpetually teazed his Highnefs for money to po-
" litical writers, and for fpies planted round the Pretender,
" Though their folicitations on thefe fubjects had been at-
" tended with little fuccefs, they continued to make applica-
" tions of the fame difagreeable kind. When the feffion was

---

* Macpherfon, vol. ii. chap. 9.
† Ibid. This was about the 21ft of March 1713, a full year
after the departure of Prince Eugene. Their objects were to
prevent the peace, which was figned about this time, to recover
their places, and ruin the Miniftry.
‡ Macpherfon, vol. ii. chap. 10,

" drawing

" drawing to a conclusion, and a diffolution was forefeen, they
" manded *one hundred thoufand pounds* from the Elector, *to*
" *corrupt boroughs, to influence elections, and to return men of con-*
" *ftitutional and* WHIGGISH *principles* to the enfuing parliament.
" The magnitude of the fum left no room for hefitation in re-
" jecting their requeft. One repulfe, however, was not fuffici-
" ent either to intimidate or difcourage a party fo eager in the
" purfuit of their defigns. They diminifhed their demand to
" *fifty thoufand pounds.* The Elector plainly told them, that
" he could not fpare the money. That he had done the greateft
" fervice confiftent with his own particular fituation, and the
" ftate of Europe in general, to the well affected in Britain.
" That he had engaged the Emperor and Empire *to continue the*
" *war againft France.* That he had employed *feventeen thou-*
" *fand* of his troops againft that kingdom. That this circum-
" ftance had deprived the French King of the power of fending
" an army into Britain with the Pretender. That could he
" even advance the money, which was far from being the cafe,
" the fecret could never be kept ; and that a difcovery might
" be dangerous, from the offence that the meafure was likely
" to give to the Britifh nations *."

Within a few pages, we meet with frefh applications of the
fame kind. " The Whigs again urged the Elector *to invade*
" *the kingdom.* They promifed to furnifh him with fums, upon
" his credit, *to fave their country,* and to execute his own de-
" figns ; but with an inconfiftence repugnant to thefe large
" promifes, they reverted to their former demands of money
" from his Highnefs. They afked penfions *for poor confcientious*
" *Lords who were in want of fubfiftence.* They demanded, with
" the moft vehement entreaties, *two thoufand pounds,* to carry
" the elections for *the Common Council of London.* They repre-
" fented, that, with that fum, they could chufe their own crea-
" tures, and terrify the Queen and parliament with remon-
" ftrances and addreffes throughout the winter †." It is not
furprifing that Mr. Macpherfon is a moft unpopular hiftorian.

---

* Macpherfon, vol. ii, chap. 10. † Ibid.

But

But the facts which he has advanced are unqueftionably true.
The original correfpondence of the parties is ftill extant in their
own hand writing. Let us proceed, therefore, with a few farther extracts from this authentic and inftructive author. " A
" propofal made by the Baron de Bernftorff, Prefident of the
" Elector's Council, was received by Marlborough and Cado-
" gan with eagernefs and joy. He infinuated, that his Electoral
" Highnefs might be induced to borrow to the extent of *twenty*
" *thoufand pounds* from his friends in Britain. This fum was
" to be laid out on the *poor Lords*, and *the Common Council of*
" *London*, during the three years the parliament was to fit.
" The firft would be thus enabled to vote according to their
" *principles;* the latter might ply the Government, and harafs
" the Queen and her minifters with remonftrances in favour of
" civil liberty and *the Proteftant fucceffion*. Marlborough and
" Cadogan undertook to furnifh the money on the obligation
" of his Electoral Highnefs, provided the intereft of five *per*
" *cent. fhould be regularly paid.* But his Highnefs would give
" no obligation either for the principal or intereft. He how-
" ever fignified to his agents, that his friends fhould advance
" the money, as they might be certain of being reimburfed as
" foon as his Highnefs, or the Electrefs his mother, fhould
" come to the throne *." It does not appear that his friends
" chofe to advance their money on this promife. On the 20th
of March 1714, George made anfwer to fome frefh demands
" of money for poor Lords, Common Councils, bribery of
" members, and private penfions, that *he would hear* NO MORE
" OF THAT AFFAIR. That, from the narrownefs of his own
" income, he could not enter upon thefe heads, into any com-
" petition with his antagonift, the Lord Treafurer. But that,
" *except in the article of expences*, he was willing to fupport, to
" the utmoft, their party +." It would be idle to fuppofe that
one part of the ifland was lefs corrupted than another. In July
1713, " the Duke of Argyle told Halifax, that *with twenty*
" *thoufand pounds*, he would anfwer for all the elections in

---

* Macpherfon, vol. ii, chap. 19.     + Ibid.

" Scotland."

" Scotland *." The reason assigned for refusing these applications, was clear and satisfactory. A letter from the Court of
Hanover contains these words :—" The Elector cannot give the
" money demanded for the elections. Besides, he should fail
" infallibly, as the Court *would always have the heaviest*
" *purse* †."

Nothing is more surprising, than the inaccuracy which
abounds in many, even of our best historians. There cannot
be stronger proofs imagined of the corruption of both Houses
of Parliament, than what have been just now produced. Yet,
with this blaze of evidence before his eyes, the writer of the
Memoirs of Britain has advanced a very strange assertion.—
When speaking of Mr. Duncombe's acquittal in the House of
Peers, in 1695, he adds, " For the honour of the House of
" Lords, *this is the only instance in English history*, in which
" the distribution of private money was suspected to have had
" influence with a number of Peers‡."

After such a specimen of the honesty of the Whigs it would
be unnecessary to enumerate all the other methods which they
fell upon to embarass their unfortunate Queen. One of their
schemes was, to bring over the Elector Prince, under the title
of the Duke of Cambridge, as a head to their party. But un-
luckily this project was equally disagreeable to the Elector of
Hanover and to the Queen. In a letter to George, dated 30th
May 1714, " I am determined," says Anne, " to oppose a
" project so contrary to my royal authority, however fatal the
" consequences may be §." And George himself absolutely refused every proposal of this kind. " His refusal was so peremp-
" tory, that the Whigs, and even his servants, made no scruple
" of ascribing his conduct to *a jealousy of his own son* ||." It
has been said, a thousand times over, that George the First en-
tertained the most violent suspicion as to the legitimacy of his

---

* Macpherson's State Papers, vol. ii. p. 498.
† Ibid. p. 497.
‡ Memoirs of Britain, vol. ii. part 3d, Book iv.
§ State Papers, vol. ii. p. 621.
|| Macpherson, vol. ii. chap. 10.

fon; and that his jealoufy was fatal to the life of a Swedifh nobleman. His wife, the Princefs of Zell, was at this very time
in confinement for her amours ; and in this fituation the unhappy
woman died, after a melancholy captivity of thirty-fix years.

Another modeft contrivance to harafs the Queen, deferves
peculiar notice. On the 8th of April 1714, " it was propofed
" to requeft her Majefty to iffue a proclamation, fetting a price
" *on her brother's head*. The Tory Lords reprefented, that the
" motion was as inconfiftent with common humanity, as it was
" repugnant to the Chriftian religion ; that to fet a price on
" any man's head, was to encourage affaffination by public au-
" thority ; and that fhould ever the cafe come before them, as
" peers and judges, they would think themfelves bound, in
" juftice, honour, and confcience, to condemn fuch an action
" as murther. The Whigs *argued upon the ground of* EXPEDI-
" ENCY *." The motion was rejected.

The Whigs did not always confine their operations to bribery.
We may comprehend from what follows, the genuine character
of fome of their principal leaders. In 1694, William planned
an expedition againft Breft. The particulars were betrayed to
James the Second, in a letter from Marlborough, where he complains that Admiral Ruffel was not fufficiently hearty in the
caufe of the exiled. In confequence of this act of treachery,
the Englifh forces were repulfed on their landing at Breft. Six
hundred were flain, and many wounded ; one Dutch frigate was
funk after lofing almoft her whole crew. Another example
may ferve to fhow the character of thefe leaders in a proper
light. In 1695, Sir John Fenwick, a Major-General, had been
engaged with Penn, the founder of Philadelphia, and others,
in a project for a rebellion in England, and had, on its difcovery, fled. Some time after he returned, was found out, and
arrefted. To fave his life, he tranfmitted to the King an account of the treafonable correfpondence of Godolphin, Marlborough, Ruffel, and many other *Whigs of diftinction* with
James. His accufation " is now known to have been in all

---

* Macpherfon, vol. ii. chap. 10.

" points true ;" and] as there was only one evidence againſt him, " he could not be convicted in *a court of law*, which re-
" quired two." But the perfons whom he had accufed, " be-
" lieved that they could not be fafe a: *long as he lived*." A
bill of attainder was therefore brought in againſt him, and
Ruffel appeared at the head of the profecution. The fequel
produced a crowd of proceedings " which exceeded the injuſ-
" tice of the worſt precedents in the worſt times of Charles the
" Second and his fucceffor ;" and the whole were vindicated by
Burnet, in a long fpeech. The bill paffed both houfes by a nar-
row majority ; and on the 28th of January 1696, Fenwick was
beheaded on Tower-hill, " *without evidence or law.*" Lady
Fenwick attempted to bribe a perfon whofe teftimony fhe
dreaded, to fly the kingdom: The accufers prevailed on this
wretch to place people behind a curtain to overhear the offer ;
" and this attempt of a wife to fave her hufband's life from dan-
" ger, *was turned into an evidence of his guilt* \*." Thefe are the
words of a hiftorian, who is himfelf a profeffed Whig, who has
been a lawer, and is now a Judge. It is difficult to fay, whether the conduct of the parliament, who paffed fuch a fentence,
or of his Majefty who figned it, was moſt completely inde-
feacible.

On the 1ſt of Auguſt 1714, Queen Anne died ; and as much
has been faid in praife of her virtues, a fhort account of a tranf-
action conducted by her Tory parliament is here inferted, which
in part is abridged from the Anecdotes of the Earl of Chatham.

It has been told by many hiftorians, that for four years,
Queen Anne gave an hundred thoufand pounds *per annum* out
of her civil lift, to fupport the war againſt France ; and hence
they deduce an argument of the œconomy and patriotifm of that
Princefs.—But, on the 25th of June 1713, her Majefty acquainted the Commons that fhe had contracted a very large
debt upon the revenues of the civil lift; and fhe fpecified that
this deficiency amounted in Auguſt 1710, to four hundred thoufand pounds.—Mr Smith, one of the tellers in the Exchequer,

---

\* Memoirs of Britain, vol. ii. part 3. book 7.

wha

who feems to have been too honeft a man for his office, arofe
and informed the Houfe, that the eftimate of this debt was to
him aftonifhing; as at the time pointed out, he could affirm,
that the debt amounted to little more than an hundred thoufand
pounds. Other members undertook to prove, that the funds
affigned to her Majefty for feven hundred thoufand pounds *per
annum*, had produced *eight* hundred thoufand pounds, fo that in
the courfe of eleven years, her Majefty had received eleven hundred thoufand pounds of an *overplus*, and after deducing the
pretended *gift* of four hundred thoufand pounds, fhe had ftill
*feven hundred thoufand pounds fterling* of the public money in her
pocket. Though this was the fame virtuous affembly which
had expelled Walpole from bribery, thefe obfervations could not
obtain attention; fince the very next day the Houfe voted five
hundred and ten thoufand pounds for payment of this debt.
" This," adds the hiftorian, " is the truth, and the whole truth
" of that generous exploit of the daughter of James the Se-
" cond. It was a mean trick, by which the nation was cheated
" of four hundred thoufand pounds *." He fhould have faid,
five hundred and ten thoufand pounds, for that was the exact
fum granted.

It is entertaining to remark the ftyle in which a courtier
fometimes talks of his fovereign. When William, in a fit of
defpondency, had once threatened to refign the crown of England, " Does he fo?" faid Sunderland, " there is Tom of
" Pembroke," (meaning Lord Pembroke) " who is as good a
" block of wood *as a king can be cut out of*. We will fend for
" him, and make *him* our King †." To the fame purpofe the
Princefs of Wales, in 1753, expreffed herfelf as to George the
Second, in a converfation with Mr. Dodington. " She faid,
" with great warmth, that when they talked to her of the
" King, fhe loft all patience, for fhe knew *it was nothing*: that
" in thefe great points fhe reckoned the King no more *than one
" of the trees we walked by*, or fomething more inconfiderable
" which fhe named, but that it was their pufillanimity *which*

---

* Anecdotes of the Earl of Chatham, vol. ii. p. 50.
† Memoirs of Great Britain, vol. ii. part 3. book 7.

" *would*

" *would make an end of them*."—" She faid, that if they talked
" of the King, fhe was out of patience ; it was as if they fhould
" tell her, that her little Harry below would not do what
" was proper for him ; that juft fo the King would *fputter* and
" *make a buftle,* but when they told him that it *muft* be done
" from the neceffity of his fervice, he muft do it, *as little Harry*
" *muft,* when fhe came down \*."

---

## CHAP. VIII.

I am no orator as Brutus is,
To ftir men's blood ; I only fpeak right on,
*I tell you thet which you yourfelves do know.*

SHAKESPEARE.

THE hiftory of England has been continued in the laft
chapter, to the beginning of the difaftrous but memorable
reign of George the Firft, We fhall clofe this part of the work
with fome general obfervations on the civil lift.

" There we find places piled on places, to the height of the
" tower of Babel. There we find a mafter of the houfehold,
" treafurer of the houfehold, comptroller of the houfehold,
" cofferer of the houfehold, deputy-cofferer of the houfehold,
" clerks of the houfehold, clerks comptrollers of the houfehold,
" clerks comptrollers deputy-clerks of the houfehold, office
" keepers, chamber-keepers, neceffary-houfe-keepers, purvey-
" ors of bread, purveyors of wine, purveyors of fifh, purvey-
" ors of butter and eggs, purveyors of confectionary, deli-
" verers of greens, coffee-women, fpicery-men, fpicery men's
" affiftant-clerks, ewry-men, ewry-men's affiftant-clerks, kitch-
" en-clerks - comptrollers, kitchen - clerk - comptroller's firft
" clerks, kitchen clerk-comptroller's junior clerks, yeomen

---

\* Dodington's Diary, p. 205, and 213,

" of

" of the mouth, under yeomen of the mouth, grooms, grooms
" children, paftry-yeomen, harbingers, harbingers yeomen,
" keepers of ice houfes, cart-takers, cart-takers grooms, bell-
" ringers, cock and cryer, table-deckers, water engine turners,
" ciftern cleaneis, keeper of fire buckets, and a thoufand or
" two more of the fame kind, which if I were to fet down, I
" know not who would take the trouble of reading them over.
" Will any man fay, and keep his countenance, that one in one
" hundred of thefe hangers-on is of any real ufe?—Cannot our
" King have a poached egg for his fupper, unlefs he keeps a
" purveyor of eggs, and his clerks, and his clerk's deputy-
" clerks, at an expence of 500l. a year? while the nation is
" finking in a bottomlefs ocean of debt? Again, who are they,
" the yeomen of the mouth? and who are the under-yeomen
" of the mouth? What is their bufinefs? What is it
" to yeoman a King's mouth? What is the neceffity for a
" cofferer, where there is a treafurer? And, where there is
" a cofferer, what occafion for a deputy-cofferer? Why a
" neceffary-houfe keeper? cannot a King have a water-clofet,
" *and keep the key of it in his own pocket?* And my little cock
" and cryer, what can be his poft? Does he come under the
" King's chamber window, and call the hour, mimicking the
" crowing of the cock? This might be of ufe before clocks
" and watches, efpecially repeaters, were invented; but feems
" as fuperfluous now, as the deliverer of greens, the coffee-
" women, fpicery men's affiftant-clerks, the kitchen-comptrol-
" ler's firft clerks and junior clerks, the groom's children, the
" harbinger's yeomen, &c. Does the maintaining fuch a mul-
" titude of idlers fuit the prefent ftate of our finances? When
" will frugality be neceffary, if not now? Queen Anne gave
" an hundred thoufand pounds a year to the public fervice *.
" We pay debts on the civil lift of fix hundred thoufand pounds
" in one article, *without afking how there comes to be a defi-*
" *ciency* †."

---

* The reader is already acquainted with the progrefs and termination of this act of royal munificence.
† Political Difquifitions, vol. ii. p. 128.

The

The following converſations on the ſame ſubjeɛt, between the late Princeſs of Wales and Mr. Dodington, cannot fail to excite the attention and ſurpriſe of every reader. "She," the Princeſs, "ſaid, that notwithſtanding what I had mentioned of
" the King's kindneſs to the children and civility to her, *thoſe*
" *things did not impoſe upon her*—that there were other things
" which ſhe could not get over, ſhe wiſhed the King was leſs
" civil, and that he put leſs of *their* money into his own pocket:
" that he got full thirty thouſand pounds *per annum*, by the
" poor Prince's death.—If he would but have given them the
" Dutchy of Cornwall to have paid his debts, it would have
" been ſomething. Sould reſentments be carried beyond the
" grave ? Should the innocent ſuffer ? Was it becoming ſo
" great a King *to leave his ſons debts unpaid ?* and ſuch incon-
" ſiderable debts ? I aſked her, what ſhe thought they might
" amount to ? She anſwered, ſhe had endeavoured to know as
" near as a perſon could properly inquire, who, not having it
" in her power, could not pretend to pay them, She thought,
" that to the tradeſmen and ſervants they did not amount to
" ninety thouſand pounds ; that there was ſome money owing to
" the Earl of Scarborough, and that there was, abroad, a debt of
" about ſeventy thouſand pounds. That this hurt her exceed-
" ingly, though ſhe did not ſhew it. I ſaid that it was im-
" poſſible to new-make people ; the King could not, now, be
" altered—."

" We talked of the King's accumulation of treaſure, which
" ſhe reckoned at four millions. I told her, that what was
" become of it, how employed, where and what was left, I did
" not pretend to gueſs ; but that I computed the accumulation
" to be from twelve to fifteen millions. That theſe things,
" within a moderate degree, perhaps leſs than a fourth part
" could be proved *beyond all poſſibility of a denial ;* and, when
" the caſe ſhould exiſt, would be publiſhed in controverſial
" pamphlets*."

---

* Dodington's Memoirs, p. 167 and 290. Theſe debts of the Prince of Wales are ſtill unpaid,

In 1755, Mr. Pitt had a conference with the Duke of Newcastle, which has been recorded by Mr. Dodington. A short
specimen may serve to show how the British nation has been
bubbled by Government. " The Duke *mumbled* that the Saxon
" and Bavarian subsidies were offered and *pressed*, but there
" was nothing done in them : that the Hessian was perfected,
" but the Russian was not concluded.—Whether the Duke
" meant unsigned, or unratified, we cannot tell, but we under-
" stand it is signed. When his Grace dwelt so much upon the
" King's *honour*, Mr. Pitt asked him—what, if out of the FIF-
" TEEN MILLIONS *which the King had saved*, he should give
" his kinsman of Hesse one hundred thousand pounds, and the
" Czarina one hundred and fifty thousand pounds to be off
" from these bad bargains, and not suffer the suggestions, so
" dangerous to his own quiet and safety of his family, to be
" thrown out, which would, and must be, insisted upon in a
" debate of this nature ? Where would be the harm of it ?
" The Duke had nothing to say, but desired they might talk it
" over again with the Chancellor. Mr. Pitt replied, he was at
" their command, though *nothing could alter his opinion* *."

The reader will here observe, that thirty-seven years have
elapsed since George the Second had saved FIFTEEN MIL-
LIONS from the civil list. It has been said above, that a sum
at five *per cent.* of compound interest doubles itself in fourteen
years. This is not perfectly exact, but as my former calculations did not require strict minuteness, the conclusions remain
unshaken. Where a topick so delicate as the civil list is concerned, the utmost accuracy may be expected, and therefore it
must here be premised, that in fourteen years, an hundred
pounds produce about a fiftieth part less than a second hundred
pounds, that is to say, *ninety-seven pounds nineteen shillings and
eight pence*, or in decimal fractions .9799316 parts of an integer.
Now, at this rate, these fifteen millions would, in thirty-seven
years, have multiplied to more than ninety-one millions and an
half. It is indeed true, as Mr. Dodington, says, that we can-

* Dodington's Memoirs, p. 373.

not

not tell *what has become of it*, or *how it has been employed*, but we know that no part of it has been applied to the fervice of the nation. We have fince paid feveral large arrears into which the civil lift had fallen, and an hundred thoufand pounds *per annum*, have been added to the royal falary. At the fame time, the nation has been borrowing money to pay that falary, the expences of Gibraltar and Canada, for the fupport of the war-fyftem, and other matters, nominally at three and a half, or four *per cent*. but in reality, as fhall be explained hereafter, at fix or eight *per cent*. Hence, by the way, the calculations as to Gibraltar are one third part lower in point of compound intereft *than they fhould have been*, and the fifteen millions of George the Second, inftead of increafing to ninety-one millions and a half, would, at feven and an half *per cent*. have extended to about *an hundred and thirty millions, feven hundred and fifty thoufand pounds*; which would at prefent buy out more than one half of our national debt, and fave the country from an annual burden of perhaps *four millions and an half fterling*.

The moft miferable part of the ftory ftill remains to be told; but the particulars muft be deferred to fome future opportunity. The civil lift is a gulf yawing to abforb the whole property of the Britifh empire. We look back without fatisfaction, and forward without hope.

Lord Chefterfield informs us, that George the Firft was exceedingly hurt even by the weak oppofition which he met in parliament, on account of fubfidies; and could not help complaining to his moft intimate friends, that he had come over to England to be *a begging King*. His vexation was, that he could not command money without the farce of afking it; for in his reign, as at prefent, the debates of parliament were but a farce. Such were the liberal fentiments of the firft fovereign of the Proteftant fucceffion.

**F I N I S.**

www.ingramcontent.com/pod-product-compliance
Lightning Source LLC
Chambersburg PA
CBHW022149090426
42742CB00010B/1431